# TORN

*God's Good Purpose in Suffering*

**Mike Leake**

To my radiant wife, Nikki.
Without your encouragement I would have never set
pen to paper. You help me rest in His goodness.

– Mike Leake

**CruciformPress**

"*Torn to Heal* is the most concise, readable, and helpful theology of suffering I've come across. The content, length, and tone is just perfect for those who are in the furnace of affliction screaming 'Why?'"

**Dr. David Murray,** professor of Old Testament and Practical Theology, Puritan Reformed Theological Seminary, Grand Rapids, Michigan

"Mike Leake has taken the ugliness of suffering, turned it over in his capable hands, and shown God's goodness and faithfulness in the midst. More than simple encouragement for those suffering, it is a handbook of scriptural truths about who God is and how he sustains."

**Lore Ferguson** writes for The Gospel Coalition, Council on Biblical Manhood & Womanhood, Deeper Church, Project TGM, and Sayable.net

"Nobody signs up for a life of suffering, but pain visits all of us. If you're one of God's children, suffering can cause you to question his goodness. What are his purposes? My friend Mike Leake delivers a clear, comforting, theologically robust view of pain and suffering. Not only does his theology give us permission to lament our pain, it drives us to the God of comfort who superintends our pain for his glory. This is a book you'll want to read when you're visited by suffering and a book you'll easily pass out to those in your world who are feeling the sting of Adam's curse."

**Daniel Darling,** Senior Pastor, Gages Lake Bible Church; Author, *Real: Owning Your Christian Faith*

"*Torn to Heal* explores God's redemptive purposes in human suffering in a concise, biblical, and authentic way. Mike shuns cliches and platitudes to help the reader put life's hardships into divine perspective and to endure in Christ's strength. It is a must-read for Christians in distress."

> **Dave Miller**, Second Vice-President, Southern Baptist Convention; Senior Pastor, Southern Hills Baptist Church, Sioux City, IA; Editor, *SBC Voices*

"Suffering well is one of the primary ways we demonstrate to the world that our source of satisfaction is Christ alone. In *Torn to Heal*, Mike Leake provides a powerful reminder of God's good purposes during painful circumstances. Read this book and prepare to be conformed into the image of the Christ who suffered on our behalf."

> **Trevin Wax**, Managing Editor of The Gospel Project, author of *Clear Winter Nights*, *Gospel-Centered Teaching*, and *Counterfeit Gospels*

"While our culture does its best to insulate us from pain and suffering, God wants us to embrace it for his glory. Mike Leake encourages us to face suffering not with stoic disinterest or dualistic defeatism, but with the redemptive purposes of Christ in view. All readers will greatly benefit from *Torn to Heal* and will be challenged in how they approach one of God's key means of growing us into greater Christlikeness."

> **Aaron Armstrong**, author of *Awaiting a Savior* and *Contend;* blogger at bloggingtheologically.com

"Mike Leake takes us on a gospel-driven path between dualism that acts as if God has lost control of his world and fatalism/stoicism that tries to bury pain beneath emotionless acceptance of whatever happens. The result is a brief but potent primer for ordinary people on the purpose of suffering."

**Timothy Paul Jones,** Associate Vice President for Online Learning, Professor of Leadership and Church Ministry, The Southern Baptist Theological Seminary

# Table of Contents

# CruciformPress
### something new in Christian publishing

<u>Our Books:</u> Short. Clear. Concise. Helpful. Inspiring. Gospel-focused. *Print; 3 ebook formats.*

<u>Consistent Prices:</u> Every book costs the same.

<u>Subscription Options:</u> Print books or ebooks delivered to you on a set schedule, at a discount. Or buy print books or ebooks individually.

## Pre-paid or Recurring Subscriptions
Print Book . . . . . . . . . . . . . . . . . . . . . . . . . . . . . $6.49 each
Ebook . . . . . . . . . . . . . . . . . . . . . . . . . . . . . . . . . $3.99 each

## Non-Subscription Sales
1-5 Print Books . . . . . . . . . . . . . . . . . . . . . . . . . . $8.45 each
6-50 Print Books . . . . . . . . . . . . . . . . . . . . . . . . . $7.45 each
More than 50 Print Books . . . . . . . . . . . . . . . . . . $6.45 each
Single Ebooks (bit.ly/CPebks) . . . . . . . . . . . . . . $5.45 each
Bundles of 7 Ebooks . . . . . . . . . . . . . . . . . . . . . . . . .$35.00
Ebook Distribution Program . . . . . . . . . . 6 pricing levels

---

*Torn to Heal: God's Good Purpose in Suffering*

| | |
|---|---|
| Print / PDF ISBN: | 978-1-936760-73-2 |
| ePub ISBN: | 978-1-936760-75-6 |
| Mobipocket ISBN: | 978-1-936760-74-9 |

Published by Cruciform Press, Adelphi, Maryland. Copyright © 2013 by Mike Leake. All rights reserved. Unless otherwise indicated, all Scripture quotations are taken from: *The Holy Bible: English Standard Version*, Copyright © 2001 by Crossway Bibles, a division of Good News Publishers. Used by permission. All rights reserved. Italics or bold text within Scripture quotations indicates emphasis added.

# One
# THE PROMISE
# AND THE HOPE

No one ever told me that an undersized 10-year-old from a small midwestern town has basically no chance of growing up to become a professional athlete. If anyone had it wouldn't have mattered though, because it was my destiny. I was sure of it. And while it was nice that my mom and grandmother seemed to agree with me, that was nothing compared to the next name I put on the list.

Lou Brock.

Baseball Hall-of-Famer. Eighteen years in the majors. Lifetime .293 batting average. Destroyed Ty Cobb's stolen-base record. Lou Brock is a baseball god.

I was barely 10 when my uncles took me to some event where Brock was appearing. When it came time for questions I raised my hand. This just seemed like a fun way to participate, but somehow Brock spotted the goofy little kid with glasses and picked me. He pointed right at me! I didn't even have a bad question in mind much less a brilliant one. In the silence, my brain racing, the crowd around me seemed to grow from hundreds to at least a million. I stumbled and stuttered and finally squeaked out a question: "What did it feel like to break a record?"

His answer was something about ghosts and them chasing you. I can't exactly remember because I was too busy checking to see if my pants were still dry. But when it came time for autographs, I *do* remember what he said. As I walked up towards him, probably looking more like a 7-year-old than a 10-year-old, he smiled and said, "Hey kid, maybe someday *you'll* break a record."

Mom, Grandma, and now Lou Brock. My list of supporters had just gone world-class. I was instantly infused with hope. *Yeah! Maybe I can make it to the majors. Maybe I can be a professional baseball player and challenge Ricky Henderson for the stolen base record.*

(Editor's Note: Mike Leake actually did make the major leagues as a pitcher for the Cincinnati Reds. The author hopes you will overlook the fact that this was a different Mike Leake.)

Of course Brock was just being nice to me, but his quip added fuel to the fire of my dreams. I took his words almost as a kind of promise—an authoritative baseball prophecy. And in my little-boy heart the flame of that promise burned bright and strong for a long time to come.

A promise from someone you trust can do that. It can shape your identity for years, or even a lifetime.

## A God of Huge Promises

God makes promises too, from Genesis to Revelation. The Christian faith hangs on those promises, and while the promise God made to Abraham was not the first divine promise recorded in Scripture, it was the first to shape the identity of an entire people for thousands of years. In fact the story of Abraham "dominates the book of Genesis and casts a shadow which extends across the whole Bible."[1] God's promise to Abram (later renamed Abraham) in Genesis 12:1-3 may very well be "the text the rest of the Bible expounds."[2] This particular promise would go on to shape the history, not merely of a nation, but of the entire world.

> Now the LORD said to Abram, "Go from your country and your kindred and your father's house to the land that I will show you. And I will make of you a great nation, and I will bless you and make your name great, so that you will be a blessing. I will bless those who bless you, and him who dishonors you I will curse, and in you all the families of the earth shall be blessed." (Genesis 12:1-3)

This promise to Abram stands in stark contrast to the brokenness that emerges in the Bible beginning in Genesis chapter 3. Then for the next eight chapters the reader encounters the fallen world with which we are all too familiar. Death, murder, pain, and rebellion smatter the pages as a pervasive corruption spreads throughout God's good creation. This is the backdrop against which the shocking declaration of Genesis 12:1-3 is cast, telling us that in the midst of all this brokenness, blessing will appear. As Christopher Wright has aptly noted:

The call of Abraham is the beginning of God's answer to the evil of human hearts, the strife of nations, and the groaning of brokenness of his whole creation. It is the beginning of the mission of God and the mission of God's people.[3]

Through Abraham and his seed all the nations would be blessed. He and his innumerable seed would possess the land of promise forever and, as a friend of God, Abraham's name would be great.

This promise to Abram, though, is not new. It looks back to the pre-fall Edenic state of mankind. This formation of a new nation is really the reformation of a new humanity.[4] The Lord, through Abraham and his seed, is fulfilling God's original promise that the seed of the woman will crush the serpent (Genesis 3:15). Our calling as divine representatives and image-reflectors to rule, rest, and be in relationship would somehow be restored through the offspring of this old man named Abram.

## Impossible Odds

God's promises often seem shocking to us. They are God-sized promises, seldom anything we could hope to accomplish on our own. Naturally they can seem out-landish, even impossible.

God promises Abraham that his offspring will be a blessing to the whole world. But God does not make this promise when Abraham is 25 and with a fertile wife. No, he waits until Abraham is childless and pushing the century mark. He waits until the child-bearing days of

Abraham's wife, Sarah, are so long past that the very idea of her becoming pregnant is laughable.

That's the kind of promise God makes—the kind that's very hard to believe.

Consider Gideon. Not only is he the "least in his father's house, "his clan is "the weakest in Manasseh" (Judges 6:15). In a line of unimpressive people, he is the runt of the litter, yet God promises to use him to lead the defeat of a strong, vicious, powerful enemy. To us, that kind of promise makes no sense.

It didn't click for Gideon at first, either, so he keeps asking God for signs to confirm this unlikely and troubling assignment. Eventually Gideon accepts that God is really calling him to do this. That's when God turns up the heat.

As Gideon is tasked with selecting his army, he starts with 32,000 strapping young gents. This was a pretty sizable army for the time, but since the Midianites are described as being like locusts in number, and their camels uncountable (Judges 6:5, 7:12), Gideon might well have wished for more.

God's opinion? Gideon has way too many soldiers.

God instructs Gideon to test his army in two different ways in order to identify the best men for the task. After the first test is complete, Gideon's army has been reduced to 10,000 men.

Conquering the Midianites with an army of 10,000 would be quite a feat. Certainly it would take the Lord's help to accomplish this. But God wants to be known as more than a helper. God is nothing less than the deliverer of his people, and the Israelites need to see this clearly. So God has Gideon run his men through a second test, a test only 300 of them pass. At this point Gideon's "army" consists of *less than one-tenth of one percent of the men it started with* and, as Gideon's Supreme Commander, God is beginning to look more like George Custer than General MacArthur.

But God still has one more change to make. As this relative handful of men is gearing up to go into battle, the Lord has them exchange their spears and swords for trumpets and jars with torches inside them. Weapons? Who needs weapons?

On the one hand this is starting to look like a suicide mission. But on the other hand there is this solemn promise from God himself: "I will save you and give the Midianites into your hand" (Judges 7:7). And God does exactly that.

The impossible happens, just like when God gave a baby to Abraham and Sarah (wait…do you suppose that when Sarah and her new baby smiled at each other, *both* of them were toothless?). God uses 301 guys (counting Gideon) and zero weapons to defeat an army of unimaginable size.

The one who makes a promise must have the ability to fulfill it, otherwise it's not a promise at all. God's promises are seldom small enough to be even slightly believable. At least, until they happen.

God is doing the same thing today. His promises are no smaller now than they were then. He tells us, "Look around your world. See how messed up it is? I'm going to fix it all! I'm restoring everything." Seriously, God? Because we seem to be surrounded by pain, sickness, violence, corruption, deception, and death. Are you really saying that?

## Assaulted by Reality

- Jimmy's frail little body can hardly summon the strength to pack up his belongings. He'll be living with Grandma now after Mom and Dad's car crash. His pain is obvious, and he feels totally alone.
- Sarah's face exudes confidence and happiness. She really seems to have it together. But underneath she is raging with insecurity, doubt, hopelessness, and pain. Each careless word slices her like a blade. Soon it won't be metaphorical; the cuts will come by her own hand.
- Marcus has dreams of doing great things in service to God. He can hardly contain his passion for Jesus, at least on the good days. But here he is again with his heart ripped out by his pornography addiction. When will he ever find freedom? Is he even suited now to serve God? Has he blown all his dreams of serving his Savior and Lord?
- Betty never thought it would be possible, but she desperately misses the elbow to her back and the constant snoring. What was once the smallest bed imaginable now seems gigantic to this lonely widow.
- Anthony may only be 8 years old, but he has to take care of his younger siblings because they have all

been orphaned by AIDS. No health care, no source of income, nothing. They feel the pain of poverty and hunger every day. His little ribs are already exposed, and he doesn't have the fluid in his body to produce tears. But he's crying. He's crying for redemption.

In one way or another we are all assaulted by reality. We all live our own heart-wrenching stories. Yet in the midst of our brokenness something within us cries out for redemption. We want the brokenness fixed. Some of us turn outward, throwing ourselves into politics, picket lines, or preaching, trying to fix things on a larger scale. Others turn inward, seeking to build our own secure little existence, walled off from the madness. At the end of the day, all of us seek redemption from the brokenness within and without.

Why is this? How is it that we can look at all this brokenness and know in our hearts that things are "supposed to be different?" Why do we call suffering wrong if suffering is universal and absolutely normal? If we have never seen perfection, why do we crave it? How can we even have a category for it?

Because God made us for himself.

## A People of Huge Hopes

Part of the reason God makes huge, outlandish promises is because he made us to crave huge and outlandish things. What we all ultimately want more than anything else is relationship with the infinite God. We want to see the effects of the fall completely and fully erased. We want to know and experience and be in the presence of perfect beauty, love, and power.

In terms of a fallen world these hopes are ridiculous and outrageous. But in terms of *who God made us to be*, they are perfectly natural. We simply want to be restored to the one from whom we were separated through Adam's sin, the one in whose image we were all created. And God's promises are leading us to the day when these impossibly wonderful desires to know him deeply and personally will be completely fulfilled.

For the believer there *will* be redemption, and there will be satisfaction. God promises to satisfy us with the only thing that can—himself. This leaves no room for small promises. A god who makes promises smaller than the vastness of our ultimate desires would be a small god, another salesman peddling an imitation. But God's promises fully match our best, highest, and innermost desires.

Again, why doesn't this match made in heaven work out better? Because we live neither in heaven nor in the garden of Eden. God's promises come to us in the context of a fallen world populated entirely by people whose best and ultimate desires are regularly overwhelmed by the immediacy of lesser desires. We are powerfully influenced by the greed, pride, and selfishness lurking in our hearts. The result is that, while we like the idea of receiving God's blessings, we often don't like the idea of God calling all the shots.

And that's where the problem comes in. You might say that all our struggles come down to not trusting God's promises enough simply to obey him. To do things his way. We want to trust in ourselves. We grow impatient with God's timing or disapprove of his methods. We want to trust in idols, false gods that promise a quick fix.

Yet God is in the process of redeeming us. The process is slow and it is painful, but God will stop at nothing to bring it about. Completely. All things, both good and ill, work together for our greatest good— conformity to Jesus. This includes our pain. The premise of this book is that the Lord, *in his goodness*, will rip us to shreds if that's what it takes to replace our idols with lasting joy. He will stop at nothing to fully redeem us. He does this by changing our desires. And this is good.

# Two
# TORN TO HEAL

A husband decides to lavish gifts upon his wife. He buys her flowers, and not just the five-dollar, grocery-store variety. He actually drops a fifty at the local florist. He stops by the mall and springs for the expensive perfume, the kind his wife always manages to "try out" in the store.

Then he finds the boutique dress shop on the main promenade of the mall where his wife had stopped a month earlier—the shop she had come out of a few minutes later, empty-handed and a little sad, yet gushing about a cute but very pricey blue dress. Before they left the mall that day, he had slipped away, talked to the store manager, and snapped a photo of the dress with his phone so he wouldn't make a mistake. Now he's at the rack, and there is the dress: costly, yes, but this is a husband on a mission to bless his bride, the apple of his eye.

He is pulling out all the stops now. He walks briskly to the mall's fanciest department store and buys the expensive line of makeup. Last stop, the jewelers. He finds an amazing necklace. Elegant, understated, perfect for her. Sold.

The man carts everything home, puts the flowers

in a vase, gift-wraps the presents, and waits for an ideal moment that evening. As his wife opens the gifts she is ecstatic, utterly thrilled. Barely able to contain her joy, she leans over toward him, places her lips next to his ear, and whispers, "You are so amazing, so good to me. And I can't wait to put all these gifts to good use."

He smiles.

That was Wednesday. On Friday the husband drags himself home from a rough day at work. But his fatigue lifts in an instant when he enters the bedroom. His bride is putting on all her new things. She is ravishing, gorgeous, radiant.

The husband takes the cue and gets himself ready, his heart soaring with love for his chosen one. After a speedy shower and shave, he puts on his best clothes and a little of that cologne she loves. Walking out of the bedroom, trying to think of the perfect place to go to for dinner, he hears the front door close. Puzzled, he runs to the door, jerks it open, looks out, and sees his wife walking toward their car, looking amazing in her blue dress and necklace. He calls her name—with a smile in his voice, but also a question.

She doesn't turn her head. She doesn't slow down. "I'm going out. I have a date." Then she gets in the car and drives away.

## Infidelity

Maybe you're more sanctified than me, but at this point I just want to scream at the woman in this story. As I consider how she plotted to use those precious gifts from her husband to entice another man, vile names rise up in my heart. For her to imagine that she is free to use those gifts for any purpose that may please her—what astonishing selfishness! What brazen unfaithfulness!

That's when I stop and realize what's really going on here. I'm not the loving and generous husband in this story. I am the adulterous wife.

This is how God's people have treated him from the beginning. Not constantly, not at every moment, but regularly and repeatedly. We take the gifts granted us by God in his lavish mercy and use them in ways he never intended. We use them to worship and serve the creature instead of the Creator.

How does God respond when his wife runs off to the arms of another? Remember, God has made a commitment to love and serve his bride, and he will not change his mind. He will never reject her. Instead, he will draw her back to himself, no matter what it takes.

In this book we will take a sobering look at an episode in the history of Israel that illustrates one of the means God uses to draw us back to himself when we have run off like a wayward bride. It is an episode drawn from the prophetic ministry of Hosea.

## An Overview of Hosea's Ministry

About 300 years before Hosea's ministry Israel's greatest king, David, ruled the land. During David's reign the promises God had made to Abraham were clearly being fulfilled. Israel's borders extended throughout the land of promise and the Israelites were a mighty people. Yet, within a couple hundred years, Israel had been reduced to nothing more than a blip on the map. This was in large part due to Solomon's idolatry, which would "tear the kingdom from [him]"(1 Kings 11:11). Israel actually split into two adjoining mini-kingdoms. The kingdom to the north retained the name Israel, while the kingdom to the south was named Judah. As these two warred against one another, the resources of both were depleted. Life was hard, poverty was common, God's chosen people did not control the promised land, and the sense of God's blessing and care for them had become a distant memory.

Around the year 800 B.C., Israel and Judah formed a treaty with one another, and as a result the people began to enjoy substantially greater peace, abundance, and prosperity. Materially, things were good again, but spiritually the Israelites were following a tragically predictable pattern. Rather than turning to God in worship and gratitude for their material blessings, they turned away from him and used their prosperity for sinful indulgence. The rulers of Israel and Judah, although wise enough to join forces politically (at least for a while), fell headlong into idol worship. Even the worship of Yahweh became polluted by idolatrous practices.

It was in this climate that the prophet Hosea began his ministry. Hosea lived in the northern kingdom of Israel. He shocked everyone by boldly announcing that all this prosperity was about to be swept away. And he was right. Judgment came first internally, in the form of violence and political instability within Israel. A string of wicked, incompetent, and sometimes murderous kings brought prosperity to a halt, and several of these rulers were assassinated in office as the result of power grabs. Society was in tatters, and then it got worse.

The northern kingdom of Israel had long suffered oppression from the much larger and more powerful nation of Assyria to the north. Israel's King Hoshea, hoping to get Assyria off his back, reached out to form an alliance with the other major power in the region, Egypt to the south. Hoshea's appeal to the Egyptians infuriated Assyria. God's judgment upon the divided kingdom of Israel, which had begun internally, was about to become external.

Assyria laid siege to Israel, eventually destroying the capital city of Samaria, imprisoning King Hoshea, and taking the people into exile. This was the lowest moment yet in Israelite history. Tragically, the warnings of judgment uttered by the prophet Hosea had come to pass.

## The Pattern and the Exception

The pattern of Israel's rebellion should seem familiar, for it is as old as the Garden of Eden. God promises to bless us, presenting a vision of a grand and glorious destiny, but we hijack the vision. We reject God's leadership in favor of our own.

- God promised Adam and Eve the perfect human existence. But after being tempted by the serpent they thought they could see a better way. Believing that the forbidden fruit offered something "to be desired" (Genesis 3:6), they sought out blessing on their own terms. They were banished from the garden.

- God promised to give Abraham and Sarah a child. But after waiting ten years they thought they could see a better way. So Hagar became a surrogate mother (Genesis 16) and bore Ishmael. Ishmael was certainly not the promised child.
- God promised Moses and Aaron he would give the Israelites water in the desert. But when Moses saw how unpopular he and Aaron were becoming with the people, he thought he could see a better way. He announced to the people that he and Aaron would be the ones to give them water. For this bit of self-glorification, Moses and Aaron were forbidden from entering the promised land.

Generation after generation, the rebellion of Adam and Eve has been re-enacted in the lives of their descendants. Fallen humanity naturally wants the shortcut to glory, not the long labor of love. It's not that we are continually wretched and constantly unfaithful. We have good days and bad days, good seasons and bad seasons.

In the good seasons our eyes are fixed on what the Lord has done and how he has already shown his faithfulness. We are like David ready to take on the giant — with a stick and some stones we'll go break some bones. On the best of these days we can feel like the return of God's garden is just around the corner.

In the bad seasons we have forgotten God's faithfulness. We are more like the unfaithful spies who see the size of the obstacles before us and begin wringing our hands, as if God has never been our help and our hope. On the worst of these days we can feel like Job, sitting on the ash heap of all we count dear, barely able to remember that God exists.

But it is the undeniable trend that over time we grow weary of waiting for the fulfillment of promises, so we are tempted to turn from the Lord and try to grab control. We grow unsure that we really trust the Promise Maker. We still find God's promises supremely appealing, but at some point, consciously or not, we begin to think he is not going to deliver on them—or at least not with the timing and in the manner we think best. That's when we begin to take matters into our own hands. Just like the Israelites did time and time again, we look for the shortcut.

In Matthew 4 Jesus—the true Israel—was offered a shortcut too. In each temptation the devil tried to get Jesus to imagine that he could see a better route than the one God had offered. Would he trust in his Father's provision or would he try to acquire it through the serpentine shortcut? Would he choose the way of the cross to reign as God's King, or would he choose the easy path and reign as Satan's king?

The core issue we see in Jesus' temptation is the same one we see in the book of Hosea: will humanity trust in God's provision and plan or our own? Thankfully of course, Christ did not bow a knee to the serpent. In trusting God perfectly, he did what all before him had failed to do. Because he was the faithful and true Israel, the greater Adam, Christ can now accomplish our redemption.

All the promises God has made to us come through

Christ, and one day they will all be fulfilled perfectly and completely because of Christ. But today is not that day. We still have a path to walk, a pattern to follow, a cross to bear, a process to undergo. This is why we study Hosea.

The first three chapters of Hosea employ a dramatic analogy—as God's people we are likened to an unfaithful wife. In a desperate attempt to escape our dissatisfaction and our impatience with God and his seemingly elusive promises, we take the path of self-destruction and throw ourselves at other lovers. But God wants us to feel the exuberance of living life and experiencing his joy in the way he intended. He wants us to live in the joys of redemption. What then should a good God do to awaken his bride? What can he possibly do to replace these God-belittling and soul-destroying affections with ones that are honoring to him? His wife may think she is content with being unfaithful, but God has much bigger plans for her. He still sees her as his precious bride. How will he recapture her heart?

His strategy is surprising.

## The Lord's Redemptive Strategy

First, it is surprising that a redemptive strategy even exists. This kind of adultery is no accident or misstep. It is the result of an open, intentional, brazen betrayal in the face of a loving and gracious husband. But God will not give up on his plan or alter it in the slightest. At the corporate level, God has determined that through the seed of Abraham all the nations of the earth *shall* be blessed. At the individual level, the Father has crushed and sacrificed his own Son so that particular individuals might be joined to that corporate bride. Therefore both individually and corporately, the wayward ones must be won back. So we will be.

Second, the strategy is surprising because the means God uses to draw us back seem counterintuitive. I would be inclined to lavish more gifts on a wayward wife in hopes of winning her back. But God takes precisely the opposite approach. The Lord outlines his strategy in the heavily metaphorical passage of Hosea 2:2-13.

> [2]Plead with your mother, plead—
>> for she is not my wife,
>> and I am not her husband—
> that she put away her whoring from her face,
>> and her adultery from between her breasts;
> [3]lest I strip her naked
>> and make her as in the day she was born,
> and make her like a wilderness,
>> and make her like a parched land,
>> and kill her with thirst.
> [4]Upon her children also I will have no mercy,
>> because they are children of whoredom.
> [5]For their mother has played the whore;
>> she who conceived them has acted shamefully.
> For she said, "I will go after my lovers,
>> who give me my bread and my water,
>> my wool and my flax, my oil and my drink."
> [6]Therefore I will hedge up her way with thorns,
>> and I will build a wall against her,

so that she cannot find her paths.
7She shall pursue her lovers
    but not overtake them,
and she shall seek them
    but shall not find them.
Then she shall say,
    "I will go and return to my first husband,
    for it was better for me then than now."
8And she did not know
    that it was I who gave her
    the grain, the wine, and the oil,
and who lavished on her silver and gold,
    which they used for Baal.
9Therefore I will take back
    my grain in its time,
    and my wine in its season,
and I will take away my wool and my flax,
    which were to cover her nakedness.
10Now I will uncover her lewdness
    in the sight of her lovers,
    and no one shall rescue her out of my hand.
11And I will put an end to all her mirth,
    her feasts, her new moons, her Sabbaths,
    and all her appointed feasts.
12And I will lay waste her vines and her fig trees,
    of which she said,
"These are my wages,
    which my lovers have given me."
I will make them a forest,
    and the beasts of the field shall devour them.

¹³And I will punish her for the feast days of the Baals
    when she burned offerings to them
and adorned herself with her ring and jewelry,
    and went after her lovers
    and forgot me, declares the LORD.

Let's recall now that God is speaking about the
northern kingdom of Israel and how she had strayed
from him. The people had begun to worship the Baals,
the false gods of the surrounding nations. They had even
brought these pagan religious practices into the worship
of Yahweh. And in seeking relief from the oppression
of Assyria, Israel's King Hoshea did not turn back to
Yahweh, did not banish the worship of false gods from
his nation, and did not plead for God's help. Instead he
looked to Egypt's gods for help — when it was Egypt from
whom God had rescued the Israelite slaves to begin with!
This is the sort of thing Hosea has in mind when he makes
reference to "feast days of the Baals" (v 13), to whoredom
(vv 2-5), and to lovers who supposedly provide good
things to this metaphorical wayward wife (v 12).

So God takes severe measures to show his bride
how bad her decisions have been. He lets her taste what
life is like apart from the blessing of God, what are the
perfectly natural results of rejecting God's good plan.
God withholds his gifts and goodness, thus exposing the
inability of false gods to offer anything of lasting value.
From this passage we see three steps that compose the
Lord's strategy of tearing his wayward wife.

- He will take away the idols
- He will take back his gifts
- He will expose her

## He Will Take Away the Idols

> *Therefore I will hedge up her way with thorns, and I will build a wall against her, so that she cannot find her paths. She shall pursue her lovers but not overtake them, and she shall seek them but shall not find them. (Hosea 2:6-7a)*

In keeping with a literary style of that era, Hosea piles metaphor upon metaphor by talking about livestock. Shepherds in ancient Israel often used stone walls and hedges of thorns to fence cattle into their pasture. In many places the walls made it impossible for the cattle to break out. In some places the cattle could push through the thorns if they really wanted to, but only at the cost of considerable pain. Hosea is saying that God is making it much more difficult for Israel to break out from the safe and pleasant place in which God has placed her. The Lord is going to block her way from indulging in these lesser lovers. He is going to strip the idols away from her.

If Israel insists on continuing to run after false gods, it will either be frustratingly impossible (stone walls) or unusually difficult and painful (thorns). Or both. God is beginning to show her that she has chosen an unfruitful path.

# He Will Take Back His Gifts

*And she did not know that it was I who gave her the grain, the wine, and the oil, and who lavished on her silver and gold, which they used for Baal. Therefore I will take back my grain in its time, and my wine in its season, and I will take away my wool and my flax, which were to cover her nakedness. (Hosea 2:8-9)*

Once Israel begins to see that pursuing false gods is both frustrating and painful, God will show her that the goodness she thought came from these false gods was actually stolen riches.

Israel has been attributing all the staples of life and all her successes and pleasures to her other lovers. She no longer sees God as her Provider, but instead has given that title to the false gods who have gained her affections. In response to this treachery the Lord is going to take back his gifts.[5] He is going to remove his hand of blessing.

You and I — Yahweh's adulterous bride — must come to understand that it is God who gives all good things. When we forget, we must be reminded that all things desirable are simply undeserved gifts from the Sovereign One. Every good thing God's people possess has come from him.

When God's good gifts are removed, Israel will be without a source of income. She will have no "wages" (v 12) from her unfaithfulness.[6] Even God's appointed feasts and celebrations will be taken away (v 11). Apart from God's blessing, the things that brought her joy and comfort will prove unreliable. There will be no more hiding behind the luxury that she thought her unfaithfulness had purchased for her. Those riches will finally be seen as false. She will end up so desperately poor that she is reduced to nakedness.

## He Will Expose Her

*Now I will uncover her lewdness in the sight of her lovers, and no one shall rescue her out of my hand. (Hosea 2:10)*

At this point Israel has nothing, not even the fig leaves of the garden with which to cover herself. All will see that without her God she is utterly hopeless and helpless. Yahweh is going to isolate his bride from her false lovers, strip away all her blessings, and leave her exposed. In the process he will reveal the complete inability of the Baals to provide for her on their own. Truly these gods are false.

These are radical steps God takes. They can even be called harsh. But they are far from cruel, because the motivation behind them is nothing but love. These radical steps will be the means to her rescue. A drastic predicament demands a radical solution.

# Three
# THE HEALING BEGINS

As the first section of Hosea 2 comes to a close, Yahweh's bride finds herself torn to pieces. Her glory is faded, her beauty is gone, her riches are exhausted. Where once she attracted lovers, she now evokes only pity or disdain. No one wants her anymore.

But then we come to verses 14-15. And it's a shocker.

> Therefore, behold, I will allure her, and bring her into the wilderness, and speak tenderly to her. And there I will give her her vineyards and make the Valley of Achor a door of hope. And there she shall answer as in the days of her youth, as at the time when she came out of the land of Egypt.

Didn't see this coming. First, Yahweh's bride forsakes her husband. Now, broken and poor and unattractive, she has been rejected by her lovers. This is where you might expect the moral of the story to appear. Something like, "Thus says the Lord, do not be as my wayward bride, but remain faithful, and love me always, and nothing like this will ever happen to you."

But the Bible is not about morality tales. It is not a set of guidelines for manipulating God into liking you, or a collection of dire warnings against doing things that would make God hate you, or a maze of mysterious tips and techniques for showing you how to "live successfully." No. The Bible unfolds the greatest conceivable drama. It is an infinitely epic tale of extravagant, sacrificial love by an impossibly patient God—love for a weak and helpless people to whom he has made a solemn and unchangeable commitment to bless beyond all imagination.

This is why verse 14 is not the point where God wags his finger at us in disapproval. It is the point where he pours out love on an undeserving bride who—wretched and broken, miserable and naked—is finally ready to receive it.

## He Loves Her

It can seem beneath the dignity of the Sovereign One, but the picture in Hosea 2:14-15 is of the Lord of the universe acting like a junior high boy trying to attract the cute girl from science class. He's going to win her if it's the last thing he does. The entire force of the godhead is committed to it.

So he finds her there in the wilderness. She is broken, naked, and ashamed. Does he run toward her? Is it a slow and stately walk? We do not know. But we can likely infer that when he reaches his broken bride, he positions his lips toward her ear. And here he whispers the kind of tender words only husbands and wives know. She has nothing left to be desirable yet the husband whispers to her, "I still want you. You're still mine. I know what you've done. I know you have nothing to offer, but I still want you as my own."

We do not know her response on that day in the wilderness. Did she want to run away? Did she wish she had makeup to mask her pitiful condition? Did she try to hide? Or did she just sit there awestruck that, after all she had done, he still loved her?

This romance always stirs my heart, probably because it is also my story. If you are a Christian it is inevitably, to one degree or another, your story as well. We are the unfaithful. And time and again the Lord has called us back into the wilderness, our wounds aching and our spirits feeble, to love us once again. To draw us back to himself. To demonstrate that his commitment to us is deeper, stronger, and more persistent than our sin.

Fundamentally, this is a picture of what happens in the gospel.

## The Gospel in Hosea

Let's back up and look at the larger story Hosea is telling. Hosea chapter 1 introduces the account of his actual, real-life marriage to an actual, real-life prostitute named Gomer. Not "just" an adulterous wife, as awful as that is. It becomes clear later in Hosea that Gomer was, to put it bluntly, a whore. She offered sex for money.

How did this prophet of the Most High come to marry such a woman? Because God told him to.

As the book of Hosea opens, God tells him, "Go, take to yourself a wife of whoredom and have children of whoredom" (Hosea 1:2). And Hosea obeys the Lord. The second and third chapters of Hosea then present extended parallels between Hosea's unfaithful wife and the unfaithful bride of Yahweh.

In Hosea 3 we find that Gomer has fallen so low that she can't even support herself as a prostitute, so she has sold herself into slavery in order to survive. If Hosea wants her now, he must buy back his own wife. Although she was rightly his bride, he still has to pay "fifteen shekels of silver and a homer and a lethech of barley" to get her back (Hosea 3:2). In that time, the price of redeeming a slave was thirty shekels of silver, not fifteen and some barley. It seems that Hosea has bankrupted himself to get his wife back.

Let's take a moment to tease out the parallels here. We don't want to miss the message of Hosea.

Like Gomer, you and I have hearts given to rebellious idolatry. It is a desperate tragedy that we tend to hate what we should love and love what we should hate. All of us.

This is a steep fall from where we started. God lovingly created humanity in his image for the purpose of displaying his glory through our enjoyment of him. We were created to enjoy God and extend his glory throughout creation. Being image-bearers of God means we have great value, but it also means we have great responsibility. The Scriptures proclaim that humanity has failed in our divine calling. We rebelled by choosing to worship creation rather than the Creator.

As a result of our rebellion we are ultimately robbed of our true humanity. We have forfeited the promises and blessings that accompany life in God's Edenic paradise. In the place of life, freedom, and joy, we are now spiritually dead, enslaved, and under the wrath of God.

But God has lovingly acted to rescue and restore us. Where Hosea gave everything he had to win back his prostitute wife, the Father sacrificed his only begotten Son to save us. Fifteen shekels and some barley bought back Gomer, and for thirty shekels of silver the Son of Man was betrayed into the hands of sinful men. He took the harlot's punishment. He endured the result of our rebellion, namely the wrath of God. At the moment of purchase, a transfer took place. The life, death, and resurrection of Jesus Christ was the price for our redemption. Therefore the Bride of Christ, individually and collectively, no longer belongs to another, but to her true husband.

The story of Hosea and Gomer points to the initial rescue that God provides for us through Jesus Christ. That is the *already* component to this story. There is a very real sense in which every believer has been bought back and we are betrothed to the Lord. A decisive blow has been dealt and we no longer belong to another man (Hosea 3:3).

At the very same time, this story speaks to our ongoing redemption, the *not yet*. In this ongoing process, God's redemption of us is active, but we are still working out our salvation (Philippians 2:12), and it's difficult. We grow weary, struggle with idolatry, and give in to temptation. We are already and actually redeemed, yet we are still in the process of being fully redeemed. Certain, complete, and final healing has been granted to us as our inevitable and eternal destiny, but the healing itself has only begun, and is obviously far from complete. In the outworking of our redemption, one of the means God uses for our greatest good is the furnace of suffering.

## First the Suffering, Then the Song

When I was fifteen years old my dad took a pretty solid blow to the head while playing softball. When the headache didn't go away after a couple of days, he went to the doctor. He was diagnosed with a slowly seeping brain aneurysm, an extremely serious situation, and was taken directly to the hospital for immediate surgery.

We were told the surgery was so risky my father might never regain full consciousness, and if he did he might never be the same person. In fact, there was only a small chance he would recover completely without ill effects.

For eight hours the doctors fought to save his life. And not once did any of us consider bursting through the doors of the operating room to halt the surgery because we didn't like what was going on. We knew that the only hope for my father's condition was the trauma of surgery. My father had to be radically and deeply wounded in order to be made well.

The softball injury actually saved my dad's life. Turns out the blow to his head caused his pre-existing aneurysm to seep instead of burst. God also worked through the doctors to preserve my dad's life. Though the odds were against him, he emerged from the surgery with little to no lingering issues from the aneurysm.

When something has gone wrong with us, we know that sometimes the only possible path to greater joy is the path of suffering. This is not a foreign concept when it comes to the physical. It ought not to be a foreign concept when it comes to the spiritual. For something has indeed gone wrong in the deepest part of our nature—radically, horribly, fatally wrong. This kind of problem can be remedied only through suffering, and to put us on the path to complete healing, Christ suffered unimaginably. Now, as part of our ongoing process of redemption we can, will, and must face suffering ourselves. Not to purchase or secure our redemption—Christ did that perfectly and completely, once and for all—but to cooperate and participate with him in the process of our daily, incremental redemption. This suffering is not "something strange" (1 Peter 4:12), but normal and necessary.

The book of Zephaniah offers an interesting illustration of this truth. The first two and half chapters are packed tight with some of the most terrifying language of judgment to be found anywhere in Scripture. In God's prophetic promises we see Judah suffering the coming judgment for its rebellion, and we are given a glimpse of ultimate future suffering and judgment when God pours out his wrath on the earth for mankind's collective rebellion. The suffering, pain, and distress depicted in these verses is, to say the least, extreme.

Then, in one of the Bible's most notable whiplash moments, everything changes as we come to Zephaniah 3:17, "The LORD your God is in your midst, a mighty one who will save; he will rejoice over you with gladness; he will quiet you by his love; he will exult over you with loud singing." It's one of those verses you see on a coffee mug or the halls of a Christian college dormitory. Redemption brings joy to God's heart and blessing to us. But how often do we remember that the song only comes after the suffering?

The Bible holds out a theology of suffering that has a good and sovereign God standing over every second of our pain, going through it with us, and ultimately bringing us out on the other side with more lasting joy in himself. The goal is eternal joy that comes through full redemption. Some day we will be healed completely and our Healer will rejoice over us and sing songs of joy and laughter. But before the song, we have to suffer under the knife. Rejoicing is limited while sin and judgment remain. But on that day when the Lord takes away the judgments against us and restores our fortunes before our eyes, there will be glorious singing and dancing (Zephaniah 3:14-16). And it will have come through the inevitability of suffering—first and foremost the definitive suffering of our Savior, but with it, necessarily, the participatory suffering of each and every one of his adopted children.

## Four
# DOES GOD REALLY TEAR?

The suffering that happened to God's people in the day of Hosea clearly resulted from their sin. God brought Gomer (representing Israel) into a desperately low and painful place, as a direct result of her sin and idolatry, so that she would once again be able to receive the love of her husband. Her suffering was a form of loving discipline that came directly from God for her good, and it presaged the suffering the northern kingdom would undergo in exile.

At this point, three qualifications are in order.

1. I am not saying that Scripture teaches that *all* our suffering is the direct result of our personal sin. The book of Job, for example, makes this point clearly. We often suffer simply because we live in a fallen world.
2. I am not saying that God *punishes* Christians. Under the New Covenant, all the punishment for our sin was borne by Christ. Our suffering, therefore, does

not come to us as divine punishment for the purpose of retribution, but as divine discipline for the purpose of godliness and joy.

3. I am not saying that every time God chooses to discipline us it will closely resemble what we see in Hosea. I'm deeply grateful that, although God has many times disciplined me for personal sin, I have yet to end up naked and destitute. Nevertheless in the larger context of Scripture Hosea does help us understand that God can and will, to varying degrees, humble us and lay us low (sometimes really low) if that's what it takes for us to see our idolatry more clearly and return to him.

# A Mini-Theology of Suffering

It can be dangerous work to try to make simple statements about the broad teaching of Scripture as it relates to suffering and God. When you consider suffering, sin, and evil on the one hand, and a sovereign and loving God on the other, you don't have to dig very deep to identify perplexing mysteries about how all these elements fit together.[7] Most if not all of these mysteries have their roots in a claim that is very clear in Scripture: God is sovereign, and everything that happens comes from his hand, either directly or indirectly.

Think about the worst thing that has ever happened to you or to a family member. Think about what you consider to be the most horrific thing that has ever happened in human history. Can you fully affirm that these events came from the hand of God? Can you affirm that everything comes from God's hand?

*Everything* includes the death of loved ones. It means cancer, burying children, and enduring the scars of rape. Everything encompasses every child who suffers from hunger or AIDS. Everything encompasses dementia and genocide, poverty and suicide. Everything means your life and it means mine.

These are obviously difficult issues. Yet no one is helped by a simplistic theology that fails to acknowledge the pain of suffering or the hard questions it raises. Similarly, no one is helped by vague or muddy theology that refuses to press into the degree of clarity Scripture offers. But we can all be helped by a theology of suffering drawn from Scripture that exalts Christ and leads to a deeper experience of our union with him.

What follows is my effort to present the barest bones of a biblical theology of suffering.

1. God is not evil and does not do evil.
2. God is executing his long-term plan to eradicate all evil.
3. God is sovereign, and everything that happens comes from his hand (whether directly or indirectly).
4. As autonomous human beings we are personally responsible for our own evil acts (that is, we cannot evade responsibility for our actions by claiming they were caused by God, Satan, circumstances, our past, our limitations, or other people).[8]
5. God ultimately does all things for his glory.
6. God is ever working all things together for the greatest good of his adopted children (and this redounds to his glory).

7. Ultimately, our greatest good is conformity to Christ, which gives us the capacity for an eternal enjoyment of God himself.

To be honest, not everything in this list makes me theologically comfortable. It's hard for me to see how these pieces combine into a picture that is both complete and fully coherent. But that's okay; the Bible was not written to make us theologically comfortable or satisfy our curiosity. The Scriptures exist for a far more important purpose—to point us to the living God who provides eternal comfort. This God, after all, is infinitely beyond our ability to fully comprehend. That's one reason eternity will be endlessly revelatory and fascinating. So it shouldn't be too much of a surprise that the God who is about the business of working out our redemption can, in our fallen and limited sensibilities, sometimes make us uncomfortable.

For example, consider these passages:

- Is a trumpet blown in a city, and the people are not afraid? Does disaster come to a city, unless the LORD has done it (Amos 3:6)?
- I form light and create darkness, I make well-being and create calamity, I am the LORD, who does all these things (Isaiah 45:7).
- Is it not from the mouth of the Most High that good and bad come (Lamentations 3:38)?

The biblical authors do not shy away from the language of causation when it comes to God's relationship to calamity, bad news, and disaster. We cannot hide from this. Behind every instance of suffering that comes into our lives is a good and merciful God. Though all of hell might use suffering to wage war on our soul, and though that suffering might be administered by the hands of wicked men, the Scriptures proclaim that God sovereignly stands over every instance with a good purpose.

The central claim of this book is that God uses the tearing of suffering to provide healing—a healing that goes far beyond the wound that is claiming our immediate attention. When we are suffering under God's hand of discipline, and then healing begins, we may understandably imagine that this healing is really all about the gaping wound we are so aware of. But God is aiming much deeper. The healing he has in mind is ultimately about conforming us more completely to him and his purposes. This is a healing that does not merely address our challenging circumstances, but also inclines our wayward hearts back to God.

Suffering, then, is a means that God uses to draw believers into greater conformity with Jesus Christ. It is a God-ordained means to joy. You can see this theology of suffering played out in the lives of many biblical characters. Perhaps the three best examples are Job, Joseph, and Jesus.

# Job
You can read about Job in the book of the Bible that bears his name. Job was an extremely wealthy man with many

children. At the beginning of Job's story Satan appears before the Lord, claiming that Job follows God simply because he enjoys health, wealth, and prosperity. "Strip all of that away and he'll curse you to your face," says Satan. So the Lord responds to Satan, "Behold, all that he has is in your hand. Only against him do not stretch out your hand" (Job 1:11-12).

Satan gladly (if we can speak of Satan being glad) wreaks havoc on Job's life. He is behind raids that destroy Job's possessions, and the collapse of a home that kills Job's children. Eventually Satan is allowed to inflict painful sores on Job. While he cannot take Job's life, Job becomes so miserable from pain and grief that he wishes he were dead (Job 3:3).

The Accuser undoubtedly took great delight in wrecking Job's life. His ultimate goal was to make Job so wretched and grief-stricken that he would deny God. But the only reason he could lift a finger against Job was because God gave him direct permission.

So you have to wonder: *Who caused Job's suffering?*

If you ask Job's friends, the true cause must have been Job himself. They claim that God is punishing him for sin, so they encourage him to repent. At times they wax eloquent. They even say things that are theologically sound, although they try to apply these truths to Job's situation in ways that just don't work. The fact is that this suffering was not a divine response to Job's sin.

On the surface you might say that the cause of Job's suffering is Satan. But if you ask Job, he would clearly tell you that the Lord caused his suffering. Indeed, all of Job's questions are directed at God. D.A. Carson aptly sums up Job's responses when he says:

> In short, all forms of dualism are radically rejected [by Job]. Job will not resort to easy comfort about this not really being the will of God: it must be the work of Satan. Of course, it *was* the work of Satan. But in God's universe, even Satan's work cannot step outside the outermost boundaries of God's sovereignty.[9]

Satan was clearly at work in Job's suffering. Yet Job finds no solace in blaming Satan. He knows the Lord is sovereign and that at the end of the day every ounce of suffering that comes into his life ultimately comes from the hand of the Lord.

There is beauty in the end of Job's story when, addressing God, he says, "I had heard of you by the hearing of the ear, but now my eye sees you; therefore I despise myself, and repent in dust and ashes" (Job 42:5-6).

Job's fortunes were eventually restored. He still bore the scars of this painful experience, yet there was also a depth to his relationship with Yahweh he had not enjoyed before the calamity. Prior to Satan's buffeting, Job had only known God at a distance. But then he saw the Lord in the midst of the ordeal, and in the end he enjoyed from God the comfort his miserable counselors had failed to provide him. In the suffering of Job God had a joyful purpose.

# Joseph

You can read the account of Joseph in Genesis chapters 37-50. Things go bad for young Joseph when his jealous older brothers sell him into slavery and allow him to be taken to Egypt. But Joseph, being blessed by God, prospers beyond all expectations. The captain of the palace guard in Egypt, Potiphar, comes to trust Joseph implicitly, "[leaving] all that he had in Joseph's charge" (Genesis 39:6).

When Potiphar's wife takes a sexual interest in young Joseph, he flees from her, leaving a piece of his clothing in her grasping hands. Offended, she uses the item to claim that Joseph had tried to rape her. Joseph is thrown into prison.

Years later, someone close to Pharaoh, the king of Egypt, remembers that there is this very talented guy in prison named Joseph. Pharaoh takes Joseph out of prison and, like Potiphar before him, comes to trust Joseph completely, elevating him to the second most powerful position in all Egypt.

Talk about a roller coaster ride. Joseph is sold into slavery, elevated to immense power, sent to prison for years, then raised back to even greater power than before. This is the point in the story when Joseph's starving brothers show up (not realizing at first who he is), literally begging him for food to keep their families alive — Abraham's descendants.

*Who caused Joseph's suffering?*

Looking at Joseph's life, you could say that every bit of suffering happened to him because of evil people who were tempted by their passions, with the assistance and wicked encouragement of the powers of hell. Yet consider Joseph's words to his brothers, about how they sold him into slavery: "As for you, you meant evil against me, but God meant it for good, to bring it about that many people should be kept alive, as they are today" (Genesis 50:20).

Evil people sold Joseph into slavery, a slavery that landed him in prison for years. But God was standing over that suffering with a good purpose. In the suffering of Joseph God had a joyful purpose for the descendants of Abraham.

## Jesus

The most evil act in human history was the crucifixion of Jesus Christ. Unlike either Job or Joseph, Jesus did not have a shred of guilt on his record. He was totally innocent, pleasing the Father at every moment in thought, word, deed, and motivation. His, therefore, was the only truly innocent death that has ever been or ever will be.

Yet they crucified him. Peter's sermon before his Jewish brethren places the evil and responsibility of humanity alongside the goodness and sovereignty of God when he says, "this Jesus, delivered up according to the definite plan and foreknowledge of God, you crucified and killed by the hands of lawless men. God raised him up, loosing the pangs of death, because it was not possible for him to be held by it" (Acts 2:23-24).

*Who caused Jesus' suffering?*

Jesus suffered at the hands of evil, wicked men. Peter even calls them to repent (Acts 2:38), affirming their culpability. Jesus also suffered because the serpent struck his heel in fulfillment of God's promise from Genesis 3:15. But ultimately Jesus suffered, "according to the definite plan and foreknowledge of God" (Acts 2:23), because it "was the will of the Lord to crush him" (Isaiah 53:10). Christ suffered at the hands of his loving Father because God had so designed things that it was by this suffering that the seed of the woman would crush the serpent's head. In the suffering of Jesus God had the best and most joyful of all possible purposes—salvation for the lost.

In these three examples, among many others, the Scriptures show unequivocally that:

- Autonomous human beings are responsible for their own evil acts.
- Satan has a hand in bringing about human suffering.
- Standing over each and every instance of suffering is a loving and sovereign God, working out his good purposes.[10]

This is true of your suffering, and it is true of mine. God's good purpose is ultimately to bring us into greater conformity with the heart and character of Jesus. The sad reality of this fallen world, however, is that such conformity does not come easy. Redemption is painful; sanctification hurts. Yet all of it comes to us from God as an act of love.

There is one more aspect of suffering we must consider if we are to understand its full scope. Conformity to the character of Christ requires our participation.

Changing the desires of sinners like you and me cannot be accomplished without discipline.

# The Role of Discipline

When I played sports in high school, my least favorite part was the strengthening and conditioning exercises. Have you ever held a basketball over your head while running an obstacle course? It's not too bad at the beginning, but after about fifteen minutes the basketball becomes approximately the size and weight of Jupiter. After that comes the thigh-destroying wall-sits, followed by more laps around the field than is probably legal.

But that discipline built endurance in us in a way that nothing else could have accomplished. As a result we could run up and down the basketball court with any other team around. If we could have only figured out how to put the ball through that orange hoop thing, we might have been pretty good. But my point here is that the part I liked the least—the physical discipline that produced endurance—was probably the most necessary. This is exactly the type of endurance-producing discipline spoken of in Hebrews 12.

> And have you forgotten the exhortation that addresses you as sons? "My son, do not regard lightly the discipline of the Lord, nor be weary when reproved by him. For the Lord disciplines the one he loves, and chastises every son whom he receives." It is for discipline that you have to endure. God is treating you as sons. For what son is there whom

his father does not discipline? If you are left without discipline, in which all have participated, then you are illegitimate children and not sons. Besides this, we have had earthly fathers who disciplined us and we respected them. Shall we not much more be subject to the Father of spirits and live? For they disciplined us for a short time as it seemed best to them, but he disciplines us for our good, that we may share his holiness. For the moment all discipline seems painful rather than pleasant, but later it yields the peaceful fruit of righteousness to those who have been trained by it. (Hebrews 12:5-11)

It is interesting and helpful to note that the discipline this text refers to is enduring—continuing to carry on in the faith—in the face of intense persecution. And this discipline is for the sake of helping these believers struggle against sin. Suffering from without promoting holiness within: this is exactly God's intention for the Hebrews and for us.

As much as we might wish it to be otherwise, it is simply true that there is a certain kind of maturity in Christ that can be attained only through the discipline of endurance. Even Jesus "learned obedience through what he suffered" (Hebrews 5:8). And if such is necessary for Jesus, then I agree with D.A. Carson when he writes, "what ghastly misapprehension is it—or arrogance!—that assumes we should be exempt?"[11]

This is why Paul could say in Romans 5:3 that "we rejoice in our sufferings." Paul understood, along with many other biblical writers, that God has a good purpose in our suffering. Tearing is often the means to healing. Suffering paves the road to eternal joy.

That truth does not however minimize the reality and pain of suffering. Hebrews 12:11 acknowledges this much when it says, "all discipline seems painful rather than pleasant." The biblical writers never minimize the reality of pain and the temptations that come with it. Again, I like how Carson puts it:

> All the correct theology in the world will not make a spanking sting less, or make a brutal round of toughening-up exercises fun. Yet it does help to know that there is light at the end of the tunnel, even if you cannot yet see it; to know that God is in control and is committed to his people's good, even though it still does not look like that to you.[12]

God in his sovereignty uses suffering for our greatest good. He tears us, whether directly or indirectly, as a means to a larger and more comprehensive healing. As we will see in the next two chapters, a biblical theology of suffering therefore leaves no room for two shockingly common enemies of our souls: comfortable dualism and stoical indifference.

Five

# ENEMIES TO SUFFERING WELL

## Dualism and Stoicism, Part 1

*Why is this happening to me?*

The question is universally familiar. Young or old, wealthy or poor, believer or unbeliever, wise or foolish, we all find it rising up in our hearts from time to time. The teenage girl who is dumped two weeks before her prom; the little boy who watches in horror as his favorite toy is destroyed by a bully; the wife who sobs through her story of marital abuse; the fearful, dejected, despondent man who after 25 years on the job loses both his income and his pension.

How can a Christian respond when blindsided by suffering? How do we prepare for those times when life grows dark and painful? Randy Alcorn explains why these are crucial questions.

> Evil and suffering have a way of exposing our
> inadequate theology. When affliction comes, a weak
> or nominal Christian often discovers that his faith

doesn't account for it or prepare him for it. His faith has been in his church, denomination, or family tradition, or in his own religious ideas—but not in Christ. As he faces evil and suffering, he may, in fact, lose his faith.

But that's actually a good thing; any faith that leaves us unprepared for suffering is a false faith that deserves to be abandoned. Genuine faith will be tested by suffering; false faith will be lost—the sooner, the better.

Believing God exists isn't the same as trusting the God who exists. If you base your faith on lack of affliction, your faith lives on the brink of extinction and will fall apart because of a frightening diagnosis or a shattering phone call. As John Piper writes, "Wimpy Christians won't survive the days ahead."

Only when you jettison ungrounded and untrue faith can you replace it with valid faith in the true God—faith that can pass, and even find strength in, the most formidable of life's tests. Unfortunately, most churches have failed to teach people to think biblically about the realities of evil and suffering. A pastor's daughter told me, "I was never taught the Christian life was going to be difficult. I've discovered it is, and I wasn't ready."[13]

Part of my desire in writing this book is to help fix the problem Alcorn illuminates: *most churches have failed to teach people to think biblically about the realities of evil and suffering*. I want to help change that. I want to see believers obey 1 Peter 4.

In the opening verse of that chapter, Peter writes, "Since therefore Christ suffered in the flesh, arm yourselves with the same way of thinking." He follows this up in verse 12 by exhorting the suffering saints to "not be surprised at the fiery trial when it comes upon you to test you, as though something strange were happening to you." Here Peter commands us to develop a Christ-exalting theology of suffering (v 1) and then to not be shocked when we actually have to use it (v 12)!

My passion is that the church might learn to suffer well by modeling deep and abiding faith in God in the midst of suffering. I want to see a church that chooses suffering over ungodliness, a church that stares down the darkness of a lost world and says, "I'll take the gospel to them," even if the only way to do that is to embrace difficulty, struggle, and suffering.

## Our Two Enemies

*Humble yourselves, therefore, under the mighty hand of God so that at the proper time he may exalt you, casting all your anxieties on him, because he cares for you (1 Peter 5:6-7)*

Peter's first letter makes it clear that Christ-exalting suffering is part of the vision God has for his church. But when I look across the landscape of Christian teaching I don't see an emphasis on that kind of faith. Instead I see an overriding emphasis on two deadly errors that have infiltrated the church: dualism and stoicism.

# Deadly Dualism

Dualism is the idea that the universe is in a cosmic battle between two forces—one good and one evil—with neither side completely able to master the other. In its Christian form, "this view is sometimes refined to make Satan either the personification of evil or the personal evil genius behind evil, in exactly the same way that God is the genius behind good…however, [in this view] neither Satan nor God is absolute; neither is omnipotent."[14]

Channeling eastern religions, dualism offers an easy and unambiguous explanation for our pain. When a dualistic Christian suffers, he or she can simply blame it on the dark side. This is fairy-tale theology, a simplistic and unfruitful worldview that replaces Scripture with a personalized adaptation of a Star Wars script and reduces God to a struggling combatant in a great cosmic war. Of course, our enemy delights in dualism because it portrays God as far less than the Lord of all he truly is.

First Peter 5:6, however, gives the lie to dualism's nonsense. There the suffering saints to whom Peter is writing are urged, "Humble yourselves, therefore, under the *mighty hand of God* so that at the proper time he might exalt you."

What exactly is under God's mighty hand? Both our suffering and our exaltation. God's mighty hand sent Abraham's descendants to Egypt and slavery, and centuries later parted the Red Sea to bring them out. God is Lord over our suffering, however prolonged or difficult, and he is Lord over our subsequent exaltation. Our calling, Peter says, is to respond to suffering with humility.

Thomas Schreiner is likely correct that, "the humbling enjoined [by Peter] probably means that [we] are to accept the suffering God has ordained as his will instead of resisting or chafing against his will while suffering."[15] A dualistic view of suffering, however, blocks us from obedience in this area. When trouble comes along, dualism conveniently turns the spotlight on that mean old devil instead of on the sovereign God and his present purposes in and through us.

But Peter isn't finished unmasking false theologies. As he turns from our understanding of suffering to how we should live in the midst of it, he addresses what has come to be called stoicism.

## Shallow Stoicism

Peter's shift takes place right in the middle of a sentence: "Humble yourselves, therefore, under the mighty hand of God so that at the proper time he may exalt you, *casting all your anxieties on him*, because he cares for you" (1 Peter 5:6-7). The Greek word here for *casting* is a participle; it helps us to grasp the proper relationship between the two halves of the sentence. We are to humble ourselves in a specific way — by casting all our anxieties on him. It is interesting that this "casting of anxieties" is set in opposition to pride. Schreiner draws out this relationship when he writes,

> When believers are filled with anxiety, they are convinced that they must solve all the problems in their lives in their own strength. The only god they

trust in is themselves. When believers throw their worries upon God, they express their trust in his mighty hand, acknowledging that he is Lord and sovereign over all of life.[16]

The opposite of pride is a simple humility that believes actively that God is truly sovereign, faithful, and good, and therefore completely worthy of our trust. John Piper explains it this way.

Casting your anxieties on God means trusting the promise that he cares for you and has the power and the wisdom to put that care to work in a most glorious way.[17]

Christianity does not shy away from emotion. Peter is acknowledging that suffering produces anxiety, and he tells us what to do about that. Stoicism, on the other hand can be defined as indifference to pleasure or pain. When a stoic Christian faces suffering, the impulse is to suppress, or ignore, or push past it. Stoicism sees emotions as noise in the system, something that just gets in the way. But the Bible everywhere acknowledges that emotions are a legitimate part of who we are, and it tells us what to do about them.

Notice that Peter doesn't say, "*If* you have anxiety when you're suffering, here's what you should do." He *assumes* that suffering and anxiety go hand-in-hand… because they do! The stoic, on the other hand, wants to deny the obvious.

So we need to be clear on two things this verse is not teaching.

First, it is not telling us—as I have sometimes heard this verse taught—to buck up and stop whining! That's straight stoicism. It errs by denying the perfectly human legitimacy of our anxiety, and it misleads us theologically by disconnecting our anxiety from our suffering.

Second, 1 Peter 5:7 is not baptizing our anxiety. It is not at all saying our anxiety is fine and acceptable.

Instead, Peter teaches and reminds us that:

- Suffering is commonplace.
- Suffering produces anxiety.
- This anxiety is perfectly natural and understandable.
- Yet this anxiety is not in itself a good thing.
- That's why God has provided a blessed remedy for our anxiety—we can cast it upon the Lord!

We don't have to remain anxious, and we shouldn't. As Christians we have someone in whom we can truly trust, someone who can carry our anxieties for us. So Peter tells us to cast our anxieties upon the Savior.

But stoicism won't be unseated from our hearts that easily. It is woven deeply into western culture and appears explicitly in many false religions worldwide. So we must consider it further in light of Scripture.

Stoics are not honest about suffering. The Bible portrays countless instances of emotional struggle, yet modern stoics, hiding behind a simplistic notion that "miserable Christians are a bad witness," just want to put on their happy face and live their best life now (more on that in the next chapter). In order to ignore the necessary and legitimate role of suffering and anxiety in the Christian life, stoics somehow cross out or overlook vast portions of Scripture. They end up self-reliant, trusting God less than they trust their own abilities to suppress their emotions and laugh in the face of adversity. Stoics are the ones Christopher Wright rebukes when he says:

> The language of lament is seriously neglected in the church. Many Christians seem to feel that somehow it can't be right to complain to God in the context of corporate worship when we should all feel happy. There is an implicit pressure to stifle our real feelings because we are urged, by pious merchants of emotional denial, that we ought to have "faith" (as if the moaning psalmists didn't). So we end up giving external voice to pretended emotions we do not really feel, while hiding the real emotions we are struggling with deep inside. Going to worship can become an exercise in pretense and concealment, neither of which can possibly be conducive for a real encounter with God. So, in reaction to some appalling disaster or tragedy, rather than cry out our true feelings to God, we prefer other ways of responding to it.[18]

Such a response to suffering is a denial of Peter's exhortation to cast our anxieties on the Lord, which requires us to be real with all the wreckage in our hearts. You can't cast your anxiety on the Lord if you aren't really acknowledging it. You have to grab it by the hand, stare it in the face, call it what it is. That's how you become honest like the psalmists. Only when you do that are you really prepared to cast your anxieties on the Lord.

In fact, in exhorting us to cast our anxieties on the Lord, Peter is quoting a powerful Psalm of lament! Behold the gritty, humble, straight-up honesty of Psalm 55.

> Give ear to my prayer, O God,
>     and hide not yourself from my plea for mercy!
> Attend to me, and answer me;
>     I am restless in my complaint and I moan,
> because of the noise of the enemy,
>     because of the oppression of the wicked.
> For they drop trouble upon me,
>     and in anger they bear a grudge against me.
> My heart is in anguish within me;
>     the terrors of death have fallen upon me.
> Fear and trembling come upon me,
>     and horror overwhelms me.
> And I say, "Oh, that I had wings like a dove!
>     I would fly away and be at rest;
> yes, I would wander far away;
>     I would lodge in the wilderness; Selah
> I would hurry to find a shelter
>     from the raging wind and tempest."
> Destroy, O Lord, divide their tongues;
>     for I see violence and strife in the city.
> Day and night they go around it
>     on its walls,

and iniquity and trouble are within it;
> ruin is in its midst;
oppression and fraud
> do not depart from its marketplace.
For it is not an enemy who taunts me—
> then I could bear it:
it is not an adversary who deals insolently with me—
> then I could hide from him.
But it is you, a man, my equal,
> my companion, my familiar friend.
We used to take sweet counsel together;
> within God's house we walked in the throng.
Let death steal over them;
> let them go down to Sheol alive;
> for evil is in their dwelling place and in their heart.
But I call to God,
> and the LORD will save me.
Evening and morning and at noon
> I utter my complaint and moan,
> and he hears my voice.
He redeems my soul in safety
> from the battle that I wage,
> for many are arrayed against me.
God will give ear and humble them,
> he who is enthroned from of old, Selah
because they do not change
> and do not fear God.
My companion stretched out his hand against his friends
> he violated his covenant.

His speech was smooth as butter,
    yet war was in his heart;
his words were softer than oil,
    yet they were drawn swords.
Cast your burden on the LORD,
    and he will sustain you;
he will never permit
    the righteous to be moved.
But you, O God, will cast them down
    into the pit of destruction;
men of blood and treachery
    shall not live out half their days.
But I will trust in you.

The psalmist is in anguish, yet he puts his soul in a position to trust the Lord. It's almost like he is preaching to himself.

*Trust in God soul! You know his history. You know he is mighty. Oh, but I'm in anguish. Oh, how I hurt. Lord, I'm anxious and fearful, and I'm almost undone with worry. But you…yes, you…are bigger. I'm trusting in you, God. I know you will save me. I know you will come through. I know I will be vindicated. But until that day, I hurt. I grieve. Yet I know you will come through!*

The psalms are real with suffering and pain, a field guide for casting your anxieties upon the Lord. They never resort to deadly dualism or try to comfort with pithy, formulaic stoicism.

A biblical theology of suffering will acknowledge the absolute sovereignty of God as well as his goodness, and it will encourage believers to trust the Lord even when he is "only dimly discerned behind events and circumstances that the Bible itself is quick to label evil."[19] When you hold to a biblical theology of suffering, you will not resort to deadly dualism or shallow stoicism. Even when your circumstances are frightening, unclear, and confusing, you will be able to exercise the faith to acknowledge God's good purpose, despite your present suffering.

Six
# THIEVES OF HOPE AND HELP

Dualism and Stoicism, Part 2

One of my biggest frustrations as a pastor is that people who are hungry for Jesus own televisions. Excessive TV-watching or the desensitizing nature of inappropriate programs are one thing. But mostly I'm thinking of the serpent venom that is so often served up by religious broadcasting

The mantra and message of these programs is that God is in the business of blessing people. The favor of God, they suggest in no uncertain terms, can be clearly seen in significant material abundance, good health, and a constant state of radical cheerfulness (at least in public). Judging from their suits, watches, and jets, these preachers are themselves blessed indeed. Somewhat less blessed, it seems, are the poor suckers who give to these ministries, convinced that anyone so charismatic, outwardly happy, and materially prosperous must have discovered the hidden key to God's heart. And way down near the bottom of the ladder of blessedness is the soul who suffers grief over his sin, and the sick, elderly widow who lives on food stamps and prays each day for the lost. Clearly, people like that have yet to fully understand God's true purpose in the earth.

These teachers suggest that God does not really use and is not fully pleased with people who struggle or strive or suffer. They would likely have been unimpressed with Paul's persistent thorn in the flesh, or with David hiding in caves and pouring out his pain to Yahweh, or even with a man of sorrows who was acquainted with grief (Isaiah 53:3).

I raise this subject not to launch a vendetta against a particular variety of TV preacher (as much as I might enjoy that), but because they represent an especially polished version of a quasi-Christian worldview that to one degree or another probably afflicts us all. These preachers show us the sort of thing that can happen when your theology of suffering comes to be characterized, not by biblical teaching, but by dualism, stoicism, or a mix of both.

- A Christian given to black-and-white dualism experiences suffering and says, "This cannot be from God, therefore it is a foe to be opposed, rejected, and defeated." The dualist has a simplistic God with a flat, one-dimensional character.
- A Christian given to self-reliant stoicism experiences suffering and says, "This is a bump in the road, an unhelpful distraction, therefore I must not allow it to deter me from my path." The stoic has a distant and

uncompassionate God, not at all a very present help in time of trouble (Psalm 46:1)

In a fallen world that groans for redemption, God has promised to make all things new. Dualism and stoicism, each in their own way (and frequently in combination), keep us from getting on board with that goal because they deny that suffering is an absolutely essential part of God's plan. When it comes to thinking about and living in a fallen world, dualism and stoicism preach a false gospel. They render us vulnerable to all kinds of false teaching, and can cripple our effectiveness in God's kingdom.

# The Gospel and the Promise

Over against both of these wrong-headed quasi-theologies is the gospel of Christ—glorious and befuddling, brilliant and paradoxical. The gospel partially agrees with each one, yet ultimately denies them both.

**The dualist believer says:** Suffering is always of the enemy. God is opposed to it, and even crushed his Son to destroy the works of the devil (1 John 3:8). Therefore all suffering is absolutely the work of the Evil One. Our calling is to overcome and defeat it.

**The stoic believer says:** God is sovereign and suffering is inevitable because the world is fallen. Clearly it was God's will for this to happen, but there's not much point in trying to figure out if he has a purpose in it. It is what it is. It will either go away or it won't. Our calling is just to deal with it.

**The gospel says:** All suffering has its roots in the fall, and God is sovereign over all things, even every outworking of the fall. Therefore this suffering has come, directly or indirectly, from God. Because of Christ's victory over death and hell, all suffering for the Christian has a redemptive aspect. Our calling is to seek to cooperate with God in his purposes in and through this suffering.

So the gospel agrees with the stoic in that God is sovereign and that we ought to humble ourselves under his mighty hand. And it agrees with the dualist in that there is real evil which God is in the business of eradicating. Yet at the end of the day the gospel proclaims (over against the dualist) an absolutely sovereign God and (over against the stoic) a God who incarnates himself and weeps for man's suffering.

It is absolutely vital to the Christian life that we hold this tension in balance. To that end I want to consider a few facets of the Christian life to try to show how a dualistic or stoic response robs us of hope and help.

## Missions

It is estimated that 2.9 billion of the world's 6.9 billion people live in what are termed unreached people groups. *Unreached* does not mean someone has heard the gospel and rejected it. It means they have little to no access to the gospel message.[20] These 2.9 billion people are unreached for a reason—in many instances it will take suffering and even death simply to expose them to the gospel message.

A Christianity influenced by dualism is puzzled by the suffering needed to reach 2.9 billion people. Predisposed to seeing suffering as something to be defeated and rejected, it has trouble processing the necessity and absolute rightness of such significant suffering. It's hard to imagine there are many strongly dualistic Christians in difficult mission fields.

A Christianity influenced by stoicism might be more inclined to acknowledge that such suffering is legitimately necessary, so I would not be surprised to find a relatively larger number of stoics willing to work among the unreached. My concern, however, is that an inadequate theology of suffering would limit their effectiveness, especially in poorer cultures, partly by limiting their own spiritual health and partly by significantly compromising the quality of their biblical teaching.

But a Christianity firmly grounded in the practical richness of the gospel will face that suffering, knowing that God has a good and redemptive purpose in every trial and every tear. The gospel exults in God's sovereignty and his power over the nations. The sovereignty of God, rightly understood, becomes an impetus to prayer and missions. Believing that God is in control of both suffering and gospel advancement, the person with a gospel-informed theology of suffering will know that in the face of 2.9 billion unreached, suffering for the sake of missions is simply essential.

# Depression

*One in five people experiences depression, and one in ten experiences a panic attack at some stage in his life. An estimated 121 million people worldwide suffer from depression. Studies show that 5.8 percent of men and 9.5 percent of women will experience a depressive episode in any given year.*[21]

Such statistics are helpful in grasping the scope of depression, but I suspect most of us are already aware of how common it is, even among believers. I don't know about you, but I frequently counsel people who grapple with depression in one form or another. Often I do this counseling in front of a mirror.

Certainly the issues underlying depression and related mental issues can be complex, but I believe part of the reason depression is common among Christians is that many of us have adopted one (or both!) of the false views I have described. A Christian's dualism or stoicism, even if they are merely implicit or partial, can cripple our ability to process daily challenges biblically. When they are explicit and consciously embraced, the dangers are far greater.

- To the extent that you see your own depression as always and unequivocally a work of evil (dualism), it will suggest to you that Satan is winning the battle for your soul. You will see depression as spiritual failure, a clear indicator that you are outside God's will.
- To the extent that you take a stoic view of suffering, then when you're depressed you will tell yourself to buck up, start trusting God more, accept your fate, and stop being so sad, you loser.

Which of these perspectives is likely to put you on the path to dealing with your problem biblically so you might actually be helped? Discerning readers will recognize that as a trick question, because the answer is *neither*. But a gospel-informed view of depression will exhort believers to fight it (in no small part by casting their anxieties on the Lord, as discussed in chapter 5) and at the same time use it for God's glory. I have found great help from these words of John Lockley as quoted by David Murray:

> If [God] had said, "Go out and preach…", you'd have gone. If he'd said, "I want you to be a missionary," you'd have gone…But because he has said, "Sit there and be depressed for a bit, it will teach you some important lessons," you don't feel that it is God calling you at all…do you?
>
> Do you remember Naaman, who wanted to be cured of his leprosy? (See 2 Kings 5). If he had been asked to do something glorious he would have been happy. Because he was asked to bathe in the murky old Jordan he wasn't so keen—yet this was God's plan for him, and it cured him. God has better plans for us than we have for ourselves—unfortunately, as we can't see into the future, we don't always appreciate just *why* God's plans are better. With hindsight it's somewhat easier.
>
> However strange it may seem to you, God wants you to go through this depression—so look at it positively, not negatively. What does he want you to learn from it? What can you gain through it?
>
> When you begin to think in this fashion your guilt feelings start to drop away. You can begin to

understand that what is happening is part of God's plan for you—and so your depression is not a punishment from God. You are actually where God wants you to be, even if it is emotionally painful. To put it another way, if God wants you to go through this it would be wrong for you to avoid it, wouldn't it?[22]

Some might think Lockley here advocates a form of stoicism, as if he is saying to just accept your suffering and trust God through it. But if you look closely you can see his position is more sophisticated than that.

Gospel faith in the midst of suffering holds a proper tension between (1) acknowledging God's sovereignty and (2) running the race with all our strength. Lockley (and Murray) want to encourage believers to fight depression through the power of the Spirit, even as we long for that day when all of depression's shadows will vanish in the light of Christ's revealed glory. This tension is only possible when we hold present in our minds the truth that, until that day, the suffering of depression is one means by which God can bring us into greater conformity to Jesus.

## Social Issues

In a number of areas dualism has overrun the western mindset. In these areas we are getting perilously close to seeing suffering as all bad, all the time, period. In one sense this is a very odd development because as a society we acknowledge the role of striving and suffering as it applies to things like business, science, technology, sports, and certain types of personal growth. No one would argue for a moment against the positive and essential role of various forms of suffering in these vital areas. Yet when it comes to social issues, the calculus often changes.

Consider three of today's major social issues: divorce, homosexuality, and abortion. I believe that each one has dualism at its root. I completely understand that each of these issues can be extremely complex. I don't mean to be flippant or disrespectful of anyone who has struggled in these areas. But I do want to emphasize and illuminate the dualistic foundational logic that is often at work in these matters, and that leads to needlessly tragic outcomes far too often. The logic, not in all cases but at its core, goes like this:

- **Divorce**: If I am unhappy in my marriage, and it seems the suffering will be more than one or both of us would like to bear, *that can only be a bad thing*. The obvious solution is to end the marriage.
- **Homosexuality**: If I am attracted to people of the same sex, denying myself causes suffering, and *this can only be a bad thing*. The obvious answer is not to deny myself.
- **Abortion**: If a pregnancy is unexpected or problematic, and seems to portend suffering, *that can only be a bad thing*. The obvious solution is an abortion.

Some Christians, when confronted with extreme errors of dualism committed by others, respond out of a stoicism that is equally misguided and only makes things worse. These are the folks who angrily lob truth grenades as they march, picket, blog, or sit behind talk-show microphones. They implicitly demand that those who are suffering simply get over it and do the right thing. Much of what these would-be counselors and commentators say may be valid and true, but to the extent that their proposed solutions are rooted in unbiblical stoicism they do not represent Christianity well and are not being helpful.

The stoic fails when he does not lovingly suffer with the struggling homosexual, acknowledge the real pain that can exist in marriage, or go the extra mile to alleviate the suffering and pain of the mother considering abortion. But a gospel-informed theology of suffering enters into the suffering of homosexuals, hurting mothers, and ravaged couples. It recognizes the deadly effects of our rebellion and life in a broken world. At the same time it resists the pressure to set aside truth in a misguided desire to make alleviation of suffering the highest good.

Wesley Hill's book, *Washed and Waiting*, exhibits a solidly grounded theology of suffering. Hill is a Christian who fights against unwanted homosexual desire. He refers to this fight when he says:

> The Bible calls the Christian struggle against sin faith. It calls the fight against impure cravings holiness. So I am trying to appropriate these biblical descriptions for myself. I am learning to look at my daily wrestling with disordered desires and call it trust. I am learning to look at my battle to keep from giving in to my temptations and call it sanctification. I am learning to

see that my flawed, imperfect, yet never-giving-up
faithfulness is precisely the spiritual fruit that God
will praise me for on the last day, to the ultimate
honor of Jesus Christ.[23]

That's really well said. Hill is neither dismissive of his
sin and his desires (as a stoic would be) nor does he cave
in to it (as a dualist would). He firmly believes that Christ
is his greatest treasure, and therefore he embraces, though
painfully, his battle for holiness.

# Prayer

Think back to your last time of group prayer. If your
church is typical, most of the prayers focused on someone's
health, or the success of some material venture, or personal
pursuit. This isn't an indictment. I am not saying that
weekly prayer for Aunt Gertrude's gangrenous big toe or
for Marcus to pass his Chemistry class, are marks of a weak
Christian. God does actually care about all those things.

At the same time, the prayers found in Scripture are
primarily about the advance of God's kingdom in the
earth. Why the mismatch? While I can't say for sure, in
general I do know that if the theology that controls our
daily thoughts and actions is heavily informed by dualism
and/or stoicism, that will definitely tend to narrow our
prayers to isolated, individualistic issues rather than
the greater scope of God's purposes. That is, a gospel-
informed theology of suffering can rescue our prayers
from both dualism and stoicism.

The prayers of a dualist are focused on fighting evil,

suffering, and everything uncomfortable in the world. That is not all bad, of course. We are called to pray such prayers. Yet if our prayers are *only* about discomfort, then something is missing.

The prayers of a stoic will not enter into the pain and suffering of victims. The stoic will pray for "strength to get me through" or "knowledge to help so-and-so accept this." Again, these are not all bad. We ought to pray for such things. But to pray without pain or passion is empty. Spouses do not talk to one another like robots. We shouldn't talk to the Lord that way either.

When we have a gospel-informed theology of suffering our praying will be different. We will pray like the early believers did in Acts 4:24-30 upon being persecuted.

> Sovereign Lord, who made the heaven and the earth and the sea and everything in them…And now, Lord, look upon their threats and grant to your servants to continue to speak your word with all boldness, while you stretch out your hand to heal, and signs and wonders are performed through the name of your holy servant Jesus.

They acknowledged the Sovereign Lord of the universe and were real about their suffering as it relates to the suffering of Christ. They refused to resort to a comfortable dualism, but readily acknowledged that just as the Lord was behind the crucifixion of Christ, he was in some way behind their present suffering. And yet, they did not pray for comfort, but for gospel advancement.

Prayer that flows from a gospel-informed theology of suffering will be real with the hurts and pain of life in a fallen world. It will be as gritty as the psalmist's cries, yet as steadfast as Job, who said, "Though he slay me, I will hope in him" (Job 13:15a). Instead of always praying, "Lord, take this illness away," our prayers will be transformed into, "Lord, use this for your glory. If you are glorified through my healing, then so be it. If you are glorified through my patiently enduring through this trial, then may you be praised."

Such a view of suffering and the sovereignty of God is what motivated Samuel Rutherford to say from his imprisonment:

> It is your part now to believe, and suffer, and hope, and wait on: for I protest in the presence of that all-discerning eye who knoweth what I write and what I think, that I would not [lack] the sweet experience of the consolations of God for all the bitterness of affliction; nay, whether God come to his children with a rod or a crown, if he come himself with it, it is well. Welcome, welcome Jesus, what way soever thou come, if we can get a sight of thee. And sure I am, it is better to be sick, providing Christ come to the bed-side, and draw aside the curtains, and say, "Courage, I am thy salvation," than to enjoy health, being lusty and strong, and never to be visited by God.[24]

Rutherford has tasted from the same stream as the apostle Paul, who said,

For his sake I have suffered the loss of all things and count them as rubbish, in order that I may gain Christ and be found in him, not having a righteousness of my own that comes from the law, but that which comes through faith in Christ, the righteousness from God that depends on faith—that I may know him and the power of his resurrection, and may share his sufferings, becoming like him in his death, that by any means possible I may attain the resurrection from the dead. (Philippians 3:8b-11)

To believers who think like Paul and Rutherford, Jesus is so precious that the cost of growing closer to him is nearly irrelevant—the price is worth it. If this price includes greater suffering, so be it. If it comes through pleasure, so be it. They have found that Christ is the greatest joy and the greatest satisfaction.

Part of the reason we are so prone to dualism and stoicism is that often we do not really believe the sweetness of God's promises. We want the comfort and hope that Christ provides, but we somehow overlook the Christ who gives that comfort. Sometimes I wonder if we really believe that Christ is our greatest good.

Perhaps that is why I have found this question by John Piper so probing: "Could you be satisfied with heaven, if Christ was not there?"[25] Do I believe that Christ is more precious than his gifts? Piper goes on to say:

These gifts are precious. But they are not God. And they are not the gospel if God himself is not cherished as the supreme gift of the gospel. That is, if God is not treasured as the ultimate gift of the gospel, none of his gifts will be gospel, good news. And if God is treasured as the supremely valuable gift of the gospel, then all the other lesser gifts will be enjoyed as well.[26]

Only when we believe that Christ is our greatest good will we be able to suffer well. In the final, closing chapter we will step back and take a glimpse of suffering from the lens of eternity.

# Seven
# FINALLY HEALED

I am a fan of the Kansas City Royals. I have saved that confession for the end of this book so as not to drive away those of you who pay attention to professional sports.[27] I am also the kind of fan who coaches from the couch, and at the beginning of each season (before it becomes clear that the Royals are going to have another dismal year) I can get pretty excited about the games.

Sometimes I have to watch a game a day or two after it was actually played. This changes the experience completely. When you're watching live, that third-inning error that allows two runs to cross the plate seems devastating. Or that strikeout with the bases loaded in the sixth surely will cost my team the game (and it usually does). But if I'm watching that game on replay, the way I respond to these things is completely different because *I already know who wins*.

If you know how something will wrap up in the future, it completely changes your experience of it in the present. Paul Tripp speaks of this perspective when he says:

The gospel calls us to look at the messiness of life in a radically different way. The good news of the gospel is that Christ has conquered sin and death, and with them every meaningless and destructive end. Our final destination infuses every word, action, desire, and response with meaning and purpose. There are no completely hopeless situations. The gospel welcomes us to a hopeful realism. We can look life in the face and still be hopeful because of who Christ is and where he is taking us. Everything God has brought into your life has been brought with your destination in view. God is moving you on, even when you think you are stuck.[28]

The Scriptures are filled with references to our destination. One such eternal perspective is found in Revelation 21:3-7

> And I heard a loud voice from the throne saying, "Behold, the dwelling place of God is with man. He will dwell with them, and they will be his people, and God himself will be with them as their God. He will wipe away every tear from their eyes, and death shall be no more, neither shall there be mourning nor crying nor pain anymore, for the former things have passed away." And he who was seated on the throne said, "Behold, I am making all things new." Also he said, "Write this down, for these words are trustworthy and true." And he said to me, "It is done! I am the Alpha and the Omega, the beginning and the end. To

the thirsty I will give from the spring of the water of life without payment. The one who conquers will have this heritage, and I will be his God and he will be my son.

I read these verses aloud over my grandmother as she lay on her death bed and I held her withered hand. The cancer that had ravaged her body had also brought much suffering into the lives of her children and grand-children. But as I read from Revelation 21 that nursing-home room was filled with hope—because Christians know the outcome.

These words, faithful and true, assure us that, for believers in Christ, our sufferings are temporary. Eventually we will be completely healed. Death and tears and mourning and pain and sin and grief will be utterly decimated by the resurrection power of the redeeming Son of God. This chapter from Revelation documents the fulfillment of God's promise to Abraham. It is a return to Eden, this time with no room for crafty serpents (see Revelation 21:8). Finally humanity will know the rule *of* God, rest *in* God, and relationship *with* God we were created to enjoy.

As I write this I am thinking of you. It is inevitable that some of you reading this book have already endured a great deal of suffering. Some have buried loved ones. Some have endured painful breaks in relationships. Some struggle daily with severe health issues. You may relate to the lingering grief of the Psalmist who wrote, "Every night I flood my bed with tears" (Psalm 6:6).

Of course we can't begin to grasp completely how much better it will be to live with God in a recreated earth with all the workings of the fall abolished forever. Maybe this is why Paul keeps it simple when he writes, "For I consider that the sufferings of this present time are not worth comparing with the glory that is to be revealed to us." (Romans 8:18). That's right, there's just no comparison.

This is one of the verses I used as my text in preaching the funeral of another grandmother, my wife's. From the pulpit I looked upon the grieving faces of my wife and her mother. I glanced into the casket and saw the remains of a dear woman who would be missed greatly. Suffering was all around us that morning.

I knew my wife was wracked by pain and grief at that moment. In the previous two years she had buried all three of her remaining grandparents. I knew she was asking questions and even in her grief wondering about the goodness and presence of God. She was suffering. Being one with her, I hurt too. I remembered my own grandmother's funeral and preaching my grandfather's funeral.

So I want to tell you that, as I read Romans 8:18 from that pulpit, suddenly the reality of the text and its applicability to very specific human suffering hit me hard. It felt like a year's worth of thoughts flooded through me in a few seconds. My mind raced over the suffering I had endured so far in my own life. I even considered the amount of suffering I will still face. This sermon had become a holy moment for me in a way I had not expected. I realized that there in that place with us was both the tangible presence of death—man's greatest enemy—and the solid hope of eternal life.

But as I looked into the casket I was reminded of another tomb, empty except for some folded grave clothes. The one who had been in that grave suffered mightily, beyond our comprehension, and all of it according to the will and good pleasure of God.

Because of that empty tomb, something marvelous has happened. Death has lost its sting. Suffering has lost its victory. It does not have the last word. And the truth is that for my wife's believing grandmother, death ultimately had no power. For her, physical death merely sealed an infinitely glorious destiny that God had ordained for her before the foundation of the earth (Ephesians 1:3-6). We may have been there in mourning, but she had only begun to rejoice.

Christ is resurrected, and with him shall rise every single one of God's adopted children. He died to give us a sure and certain hope for life beyond this fallen world where suffering awaits around every corner. This is why we can cast all our anxieties upon this suffering Savior, who knows our pain and cares for us.

So let us revisit the apostle's words: "For I consider that the sufferings of this present time are not worth comparing with the glory that is to be revealed to us." As I read that and think about the pain that can come my way in any given week, I recall that I am just one person among billions, and every one of us suffers.

But the words mean what they mean. All the rape,

murder, death, violence, broken relationships, anguish, disabilities, cancer, and all the rest are *nothing* compared to the glory that is to be revealed to us. I believe that. I'm certain there's just *no comparison*, no point in even making the effort. God's infinite glory, power, and holiness are so beyond our grasp that our sufferings will vanish like a speck of dust consumed by the sun—and even that image does not come close. The wonders to come are so infinitely beyond the sufferings we now face that you can't even talk about how huge the difference is. It is beyond our words, beyond our experience, and beyond even our wildest dreams.

*Oh, how precious must Jesus be that this is true! To consider the sufferings of all humanity and know they are nothing in comparison, Christ must be very precious indeed!*

So the Bible acknowledges our suffering, fully and completely, without ever minimizing the present reality and pain, and without ever giving an inch to the powers of darkness that ever strive but ever fail to defeat God's children. Indeed the Scriptures present suffering as a painful yet merciful tool in the hands of a loving God. Our loving Father uses the furnace of suffering to separate from us anything that will not lead to our ultimate delight. Though painful at the time, there is a good purpose of God in our suffering. He will tear us for the sake of healing us, and he will do it in love, for his eternal glory and our eternal good.

# Appendix
# TWO LIONS

It is my prayer that this book has been helpful to suffering saints and that it may aid some readers in the development of a biblical theology of suffering.

More than likely you still have questions about the relationship of God to suffering. As I said earlier in this book, I still have questions myself. I long for the day when I find myself more like Job who, having seen God in his fullness said, "Behold, I am of small account; what shall I answer you? I lay my hand on my mouth. I have spoken once, and I will not answer; twice, but I will proceed no further" (Job 40:4-5).

As I read through the Scriptures I see two lions. The first is found in 1 Peter 5:8, "Your adversary the devil prowls around like a roaring lion." This lion desires to destroy our faith. He is active. He constantly seeks to impede the growth of the gospel. If this lion were sovereign he would gladly rip us to pieces. He is a hungry lion, searching and waiting for someone to devour.

This lion represents the devil. He does indeed inflict suffering upon us. His goal is to tear us up, rob us of faith, destroy us, and tempt us to sin and hate God. The devil wants us to turn from Christ, turn against our neighbors, and become bitter, cynical, and hopeless. He wants to devour us and dethrone God from our hearts and lives.

But there is another lion found in the Scriptures. He appears in Hosea 13:7-8.

> So I am to them like a lion; like a leopard I will lurk beside the way. I will fall upon them like a bear robbed of her cubs; I will tear open their breast, and there I will devour them like a lion, as a wild beast would rip them open.

It sounds as if this lion does the same thing our adversary the devil does. Yet, this is Yahweh speaking. Hosea 6:1-2 makes clear the purpose of *this* lion:

> Come, let us return to the LORD; for he has torn us, that he may heal us; he has struck us down, and he will bind us up. After two days he will revive us; on the third day he will raise us up, that we may live before him.

This lion can indeed be violent, but there is a good purpose in the suffering he inflicts. This lion tears and wounds and does so for a good reason. If he has wounded you, I can't say I know the specific reason for his tearing. But because, through the Scriptures, I know something about the heart of man and the purposes of God, I'm confident I know the general goal.

- He is ripping out idols.
- He is strengthening your faith.
- He is magnifying the beauty of Christ in your life.
- He is furthering his kingdom through you.

This is a process that lasts your entire life. Like any extended process, it can be hard to see the significance of any single action. But over time the progress becomes clear. The lion is at work, and every tear from his paw contributes to your good.

I close with a scene from the C.S. Lewis' *Voyage of the Dawn Treader*. Here, the disagreeable boy Eustace Scrubb, who was turned into a dragon, is talking with his cousin Edmund.

> "I looked up and saw the very last thing I expected: a huge lion coming slowly toward me. And one queer thing was that there was no moon last night, but there was moonlight where the lion was. So it came nearer and nearer. I was terribly afraid of it. You may think that, being a dragon, I could have knocked any lion out easily enough. But it wasn't that kind of fear. I wasn't afraid of it eating me, I was just afraid of it — if you can understand. Well, it came close up to me and looked straight into my eyes. And I shut my eyes tight. But that wasn't any good because it told me to follow it."
>
> "You mean it spoke?"
>
> "I don't know. Now that you mention it, I don't think it did. But it told me all the same. And

I knew I'd have to do what it told me, so I got up and followed it. And it led me a long way into the mountains. And there was always this moonlight over and round the lion wherever we went. So at last when we came to the top of a mountain I'd never seen before and on the top of this mountain there was a garden—trees and fruit and everything. In the middle of it there was a well…

"Then the lion said—but I don't know if it spoke—'You will have to let me undress you.' I was afraid of his claws, I can tell you, but I was pretty nearly desperate now. So I just lay flat down on my back to let him do it.

"The very first tear he made was so deep that I thought it had gone right into my heart. And when he began pulling the skin off, it hurt worse than anything I've ever felt. The only thing that made me able to bear it was just the pleasure of feeling the stuff peel off. You know—if you've ever picked the scab off a sore place. It hurts like billy—oh but it is such fun to see it coming away."

"I know exactly what you mean," said Edmund.

"Well, he peeled the beastly stuff right off—just as I thought I'd done it myself the other three times, only they hadn't hurt—and there it was lying on the grass: only ever so much thicker, and darker, and more knobby-looking than the others had been. And there was I as smooth and soft as a peeled switch and smaller than I had been. Then he caught hold of me—I didn't like that much for I was very tender underneath now that I'd no skin on—and threw me into the water. It smarted like anything but only for a moment. After that it became perfectly delicious and as soon as I started swimming and splashing I found that all the pain had gone from my arm. And then I saw why. I'd turned into a boy again."[29]

You and I are being un-dragoned. Take heart, suffering saint, Aslan is on the move. One day the tearing will be over and we will be swimming and splashing in the river of glory!

# Endnotes

1.  Alexander, T. Desmond and Brian S. Rosner, *New Dictionary of Biblical Theology* (Leicester, England: Inter-Varsity Press, 2000), 367.

2.  Roberts, Vaughan, *God's Big Picture: Tracing the Storyline of the Bible* (Downers Grove, Illinois: InterVarsity Press, 2002), 53.

3.  Wright, Christopher J. H., *The Mission of God's People: A Biblical Theology of the Church's Mission* (Grand Rapids, Michigan: Zondervan, 2010), 66.

4.  Dempster, Stephen G., *Dominion and Dynasty: A Biblical Theology of the Hebrew Bible* (Leicester, England: Apollos, 2003), 81.

5.  Notice in v 5 how wayward Israel refers to all God's material blessings as her own. This is true, but only in a limited sense. God's blessings do not come unconditionally. They come to us with an intended purpose. Like the wife who shouldn't use her husband's gifts of clothing, jewelry, and perfume to entice another man, we are not free to use God's gifts in any way that might please us.

6.  Ortlund, Raymond C. God's Unfaithful Wife: A Biblical Theology of Spiritual Adultery (Downers Grove, Ill: Intervarsity Press, 2002) p 65.

7.  In this book I do not address the philosophical problem of evil or present a detailed theodicy (a defense of God's goodness and omnipotence in the face of the reality of suffering). I do not believe God has chosen to shed much light on that question in the Scriptures, and I'm happy to take that as my cue not to engage in speculation.

8.  Of course we do not possess full autonomy, for at every moment we rely on God to keep us alive and keep creation intact. But the behavioral autonomy we do possess is the real thing.

9.  Carson, D.A., *How Long, O Lord: Reflections on Suffering and Evil* (Grand Rapids, Michigan: Baker Academic, 2007), 140.

10. By this I don't mean that God stands over good and evil or

blessings and suffering in the same way. As D.A. Carson puts it, "He stands behind evil in such a way that none of it takes place outside the limits of his sovereign sway, but so that no evil is chargeable to him; he stands behind good in such a way that all of it is credited to him." (Schreiner, Thomas R., and Bruce A. Ware. Still Sovereign ; Contemporary Perspectives on Election, Foreknowledge, and Grace. Grand Rapids, MI: Baker Book House, 2000. pp 271-72)

11.   Carson, 72.

12.   Carson, 66.

13.   Alcorn, Randy C., *The Goodness of God: Assurance of Purpose in the Midst of Suffering* (Colorado Springs, Colorado: Multnomah Books, 2010) 5.

14.   Carson, 28.

15.   Schreiner, Thomas R., *1, 2 Peter, Jude* (Nashville, Tennessee: Broadman & Holman, 2003), 239.

16.   Schreiner, 241.

17.   From a sermon preached by John Piper, "Are You Humble Enough to Be Care-Free," accessed April 22, 2013, http://www.desiringgod.org/resource-library/sermons/are-you-humble-enough-to-be-care-free.

18.   Wright, Christopher J.H., *The God I Don't Understand: Reflections on Tough Questions of Faith* (Grand Rapids, Michigan: Zondervan, 2008), 52.

19.   Carson, 65.

20.   Cited from The Joshua Project, accessed April 22, 2013, http://www.joshuaproject.net/.

21.   Murray, David P., *Christians Get Depressed Too: Hope and Help for Depressed People* (Grand Rapids, Michigan: Reformation Heritage Books, 2010), 3.

22.   Quoted from Murray, 51-52.

23.   Hill, Wesley, Washed and Waiting: Reflections on Christian Faithfulness and Homosexuality (Grand Rapids, Michigan: Zondervan, 2010), 146.

24.   Rutherford, Samuel. *Letters of Samuel Rutherford: A*

*Selection*. Edinburgh: Banner of Truth Trust, 1996. Page 18-19

25. Piper, John. *God is the Gospel* (Wheaton, IL: Crossway Books, 2011) p 15.

26. Piper, p 45.

27. As I am writing this the Royals are not exactly a dominant team. But when you read this at some point after the 2012 season you will be wondering what I am talking about, because the Royals will be awesome and in first place and winning world championships. I'm sure of it.

28. Lane, Timothy S. and Paul David Tripp, *How People Change* (Greensboro, North Carolina: New Growth Press, 2008), 44.

29. Lewis, C.S. and Pauline Baynes, *The Voyage of the Dawn Treader* (New York: Harper Trophy, 1994), 115-116.

# Broken Vows
## Divorce and the Goodness of God

by John Greco

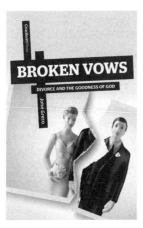

**Because divorce can and does happen, even to Christians.**

86 pages
bit.ly/B-VOWS

"'I really, really like this book...John helps us see and live in the relentless grace and sure direction of the Father in the face of our seemingly unbearable real-life trials. He writes wisely, not from untried theory, but fire-tested experience."

**Glenn T. Stanton, Director of Family Formation Studies, Focus on the Family**

"'I've always marveled at Joseph's perspective in Genesis 50:20. He acknowledged the deep pain his brothers had inflicted on him, but also recognized God's sovereign ability to transform his personal pain into something beautiful. I had the same feeling as I read Broken Vows. John Greco does a beautiful job making it clear that though he never wanted his marriage to end, he would never trade the intimacy he now enjoys with his Heavenly Father. This book is filled with wisdom from cover to cover. It's the overflow of a painful personal struggle that resulted in a life full of authenticity and hope."

**Phil Tuttle, President and CEO, Walk Thru the Bible**

"John Greco's first-hand account of coping with the trauma of broken vows offers straightforward and biblical insight into a complicated subject. *Broken Vows* provides a lifeline of hope laced with empathy, practical guidance, and non-judgmental biblical wisdom."

**Laura Petherbridge, author, When "I Do" Becomes "I Don't"**

## Good News About Satan
### A Gospel Look at Spiritual Warfare

by Bob Bevington
Foreword by Jerry Bridges

**The world, the flesh...the Devil and his demons. How do they work together against us?**

**Learn to recognize and resist the enemy in the power of the gospel.**

*108 pages*
*bit.ly/SATANLOSES*

"Spiritual warfare is certainly an important biblical topic; from one perspective it is the central topic of the whole Bible. So it's important that believers get sober and reliable guidance on the subject. Bob Bevington's book is one of the most helpful. His book is reliable, biblical, and practical. It is easy to understand and challenges our spiritual complacency."
### *Dr. John M. Frame, Reformed Theological Seminary*

"This is the best book I have ever read on this subject. I simply could not put it down. It is both highly Christ-centered and very practical, having the wonderful effect of focusing the reader's attention directly on Jesus while at the same time providing much useful help in the believer's battle against the enemy."
### *Mike Cleveland, Founder and President, Setting Captives Free*

"Filled with biblical reconnaissance and helpful insights for the conduct of spiritual warfare... a stimulating analysis of the biblical data, drawing boundaries between the factual and fanciful, and grounding the reader firmly on the gospel of Jesus Christ."
### *Stanley Gale, author, What is Spiritual Warfare?*

"Read this book, prepare for battle, and rejoice in the victory that has been won and the glory that will shine more brightly."
### *Justin Taylor, co-author, The Final Days of Jesus*

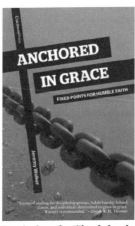

## Anchored in Grace
Fixed Truths for Humble Faith

by Jeremy Walker

**Clear truths from Scripture...**

**Central. Humbling. Saving.
Comforting. God-glorifying.**

**Get Anchored.**

*86 pages
bit.ly/ANCHRD*

"Rarely does the title of a book so clearly represent its contents as does this one. With brevity and precision, Jeremy Walker sets forth God's work of salvation in the believer from beginning to end. In a day when there is so much confusion regarding even the most fundamental truths of redemption, this concise yet comprehensive work is a clear beacon of light to guide the seeker and to instruct and comfort the believer."

***Paul David Washer, Director, HeartCry Missionary Society***

"As a pastor, I am always looking for a book that is brief, simple, and biblical in its presentation of the God-exalting doctrines of grace to put into the hands of believers. I think my search is now over!"

***Conrad Mbewe, African Christian University, Lusaka, Zambia***

"Crisp, clear, concise, and biblical, Walker's book offers up the doctrines of God's grace in a manner persuasive to the mind and powerful to the heart."

***Dr. Joel R. Beeke, Pres., Puritan Reformed Theological Seminary***

"A sure-footed journey...a trusted guide. Reading this book will both thrill and convict, challenge and confirm. Essential reading for discipleship groups, Adult Sunday School classes, and individuals determined to grow in grace. Warmly recommended."

***Derek W. H. Thomas, Professor, Reformed Theological Seminary***

## Brass Heavens
### Reasons for Unanswered Prayer
by Paul Tautges

**Does it ever seem like God is not listening?**

**Scripture offers six clear reasons why your prayers may go unanswered.**

**Learn what they are and what you can do about it.**

*112 pages   bit.ly/BRASS-H*

"Paul Tautges scatters the darkness of doubt. He blends biblical teaching with practical illustrations to challenge and comfort us when the heavens seem as brass. Read this to revive your prayers, to melt the heavens, and to increase your answers."
### *David Murray, Puritan Reformed Theological Seminary*

"Some things in the Scriptures are conveniently ignored...but this book will not let us continue to bury Scripture's clear teaching, or continue to ignore the ongoing rebellions, unrelinquished resentments, and unconfessed sins in our lives that may be hindering our prayers."
### *Nancy Guthrie, author, Seeing Jesus in the Old Testament*

"Both motivating and convicting....Read and obey for the sake of your future, your family, and the work of God in the world."
### *Jim Elliff, President, Christian Communicators Worldwide*

"Like the Scriptures, Paul Tautges does not leave us in the pit of despair, but shows that where sin abounds, grace superabounds—there are biblical pathways for dealing with our role in unanswered prayers and for responding humbly to God's affectionate sovereignty."
### *Bob Kellemen, Executive Dir., Biblical Counseling Coalition*

## Grieving, Hope and Solace
### When a Loved One Dies in Christ

by Albert N. Martin

**There is comfort for the grief.
There are answers to the questions.
The Bible does offer hope, solace,
healing, and confidence.**

**Pastor Albert Martin has been
there.**

"This tender book by a much-loved pastor, written after the death of
his beloved wife, offers comfort to those in tears. A rare guidebook to
teach us how to grieve with godliness, it is relevant to us all – if not for
today, then no doubt for tomorrow."
***Maurice Roberts, former editor,* Banner of Truth *magazine***

"Albert N. Martin is a seasoned pastor, skilled teacher, and gifted writer
who has given us a priceless treasure in this book. All who read these
pages will, unquestionably, be pointed to Christ and find themselves
greatly helped."
***Steve Lawson, Christ Fellowship Baptist Church, Mobile, AL***

"Like turning the corner and being met by a glorious moonrise, or
discovering a painter or musician who touches us in the deepest
recesses of our being–this little book by Pastor Al Martin has been
such an experience for me. Whether you are a pastor or counselor,
one who is experiencing the pangs of grief, or a member of the
church who wants to be useful to others, you need to read this book."
***Joseph Pipa, President, Greenville Presbyterian Theo. Sem.***

"Personal tenderness and biblical teaching in a sweet book of comfort. Buy it and give it away, but make sure to get a copy for yourself."
***Dr. Joel R. Beeke, President, Puritan Reformed Theo. Sem.***

## The Secret of Spiritual Joy
by William P. Farley

**There really is a guaranteed path to greater joy.**

**The secret is gratitude.**

**To strengthen your confidence in this truth, read this book.**

*93 pages*
*bit.ly/SPIRITUALJOY*

"Is there really one thing, above all else, that can be demonstrated to be the secret? Bill Farley has made his case and it is compelling. Oh, what biblical wisdom is contained in this brief book. Reading it has given me greater earnestness to pursue the path of joy Farley has here mapped so skillfully. May God be pleased to use this book to do the same for innumerable other Christian pilgrims."

**Bruce A. Ware, author; Chairman, Department of Christian Theology, The Southern Baptist Theological Seminary**

"Continuing his explorations of how the biblical gospel both fuels and shapes the cultivation of Christ-like virtues, Bill Farley turns his attention to the joy that sadly seems to elude so many believers. He interweaves solid theology with practical illustrations so that all who read this short but powerful book can emerge with a trustworthy and clear understanding of how to recognize and experience this gracious blessing from the Lord."

**Randal Roberts, President, Western Seminary**

"Bill Farley wants to obliterate our propensities for grumbling and self-pity. This may prove to be a dangerous book for those who wallow in dispositions that are antithetical to the Christian gospel."

**Art Azurdia, Senior Minister,Trinity Church (Portland, OR); Director, Doctor of Ministry Program, Western Seminary**

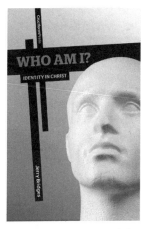

# Who Am I?
### Identity in Christ
by Jerry Bridges

**Jerry Bridges unpacks Scripture to give the Christian eight clear, simple, interlocking answers to one of the most essential questions of life.**

*91 pages*
*bit.ly/WHOAMI*

"Jerry Bridges' gift for simple but deep spiritual communication is fully displayed in this warm-hearted, biblical spelling out of the Christian's true identity in Christ."

**J. I. Packer, *Theological Editor*, ESV Study Bible; *author*, Knowing God, A Quest for Godliness, Concise Theology**

"I know of no one better prepared than Jerry Bridges to write *Who Am I?* He is a man who knows who he is in Christ and he helps us to see succinctly and clearly who we are to be. Thank you for another gift to the Church of your wisdom and insight in this book."

**R.C. Sproul, *founder, chairman, president, Ligonier Ministries; executive editor*, Tabletalk *magazine; general editor*, The Reformation Study Bible**

"*Who Am I?* answers one of the most pressing questions of our time in clear gospel categories straight from the Bible. This little book is a great resource to ground new believers and remind all of us of what God has made us through faith in Jesus. Thank the Lord for Jerry Bridges, who continues to provide the warm, clear, and biblically balanced teaching that has made him so beloved to this generation of Christians."

**Richard D. Phillips, *Senior Minister, Second Presbyterian Church, Greenville, SC***

## "But God..."
The Two Words at the Heart of the Gospel

by Casey Lute

**Just two words.**
**Understand their use in Scripture,**
**and you will never be the same.**

*100 pages*
*bit.ly/ButGOD*

"Keying off of nine occurrences of "But God" in the English Bible, Casey Lute ably opens up Scripture in a manner that is instructive, edifying, encouraging, and convicting. This little book would be useful in family or personal reading, or as a gift to a friend. You will enjoy Casey's style, you will have a fresh view of some critical Scripture, and your appreciation for God's mighty grace will be deepened."
**Dan Phillips, Pyromaniacs blog, author of The World-Tilting**
**Gospel (forthcoming from Kregel)**

"A refreshingly concise, yet comprehensive biblical theology of grace that left this reader more in awe of the grace of God. "
**Aaron Armstrong, BloggingTheologically. com**

""Casey Lute reminds us that nothing is impossible with God, that we must always reckon with God, and that God brings life out of death and joy out of sorrow. "
**Thomas R. Schreiner, Professor of New Testament**
**Interpretation, The Southern Baptist Theological Seminary**

"A mini-theology that will speak to the needs of every reader of this small but powerful book. Read it yourself and you will be blessed. Give it to a friend and you will be a blessing."
**William Varner, Prof. of Biblical Studies, The Master's College**

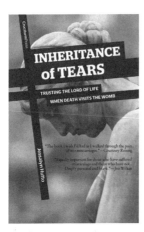

# Inheritance of Tears

## Trusting the Lord of Life When Death Visits the Womb

### by Jesssalyn Hutto

**Miscarriage: deeply traumatic, tragically common, too often misunderstood.**

*95 pages   bit.ly/OFTEARS*

"We wish there had been good Christian books on miscarriage available when we faced that terrible trial. This book is written out of deep suffering, but with an even deeper sense of hope. This book can help you think and pray if you have faced miscarriage, and it can help you understand how to minister to someone who has."

**Russell and Maria Moore**

"This book is equally important for those who have suffered miscarriage and those who have not. Rarely is the topic of miscarriage addressed with such candor and depth. Deeply personal and brave, Inheritance of Tears unveils a picture of miscarriage drawn from first-hand experience and attentive consideration of Scripture. Jessalyn invites us to ask the hard questions, to enter into the suffering of our sisters, to remember the goodness of God even in the midst of unspeakable loss. May her words minister to many."

**Jen Wilkin, author, Women of the Word (Crossway)**

"If you are suffering, I'm so glad you are holding this book. You won't find soggy counsel, glib advice, or verses ripped out of context. Jessalyn writes with warmth, conviction, and clarity, helping us stare down suffering by directing our gaze to the Lord of glory. I think you, and thousands more, will be helped by this wonderful book."

**JA Medders, author, Gospel Formed: Living a Grace-Addicted, Truth-Filled, Jesus-Exalting Life (Kregel)**

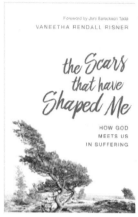

Foreword by Joni Eareckson Tada

VANEETHA RENDALL RISNER

the Scars
that have
Shaped Me

HOW GOD
MEETS US
IN SUFFERING

## The Scars That Have Shaped Me
How God Meets Us in Suffering

by Vaneethat Rendall Risner
Foreword by Joni Eareckson Tada

**"Raw, transparent, terrifiying, and yet amazingly hopeful!"**
**Brian Fikkert, co-author of *When Helping Hurts***

*Published for Desiring God by Cruciform Press*

"Vaneetha writes with creativity, biblical faithfulness, compelling style, and an experiential authenticity that draws other sufferers in. Here you will find both a tested life and a love for the sovereignty of a good and gracious God."
### *John Piper, author of* Desiring God *and many other books*

"*The Scars That Have Shaped Me* will make you weep and rejoice not just because it brims with authenticity and integrity, but because every page points you to the rest that is found in entrusting your life to one who is in complete control and is righteous, powerful, wise, and good in every way."
### *Paul Tripp, pastor, author, international conference speaker*

"'I could not put this book down, except to wipe my tears. Vaneetha's testimony of God's kindness to her in pain was exactly what I needed; no doubt, many others will feel the same. It has helped me process my own grief and loss, and given me renewed hope to care for those in my life who suffer in various ways."
### *Gloria Furman, author,* **Missional Motherhood; Alive in Him**

"Vaneetha Risner's credibility makes us willing to lean in and listen. Her writing is built on her experience of deep pain, and in the midst of that her rugged determination to hold on to Christ."
### *Nancy Guthrie, author,* **Hearing Jesus Speak into Your Sorrow**